Happy

Lots of love,

x mum x

Ken Hom
Classic Chinese Recipes

Ken Hom
Classic Chinese Recipes

75 signature dishes

hamlyn

An Hachette UK Company
www.hachette.co.uk

First published in Great Britain in 2011 by
Hamlyn, a division of Octopus Publishing Group Ltd
Endeavour House
189 Shaftesbury Avenue
London
WC2H 8JY
www.octopusbooks.co.uk

ISBN 978-0-600-62077-8

A CIP catalogue record for this book is available from the British Library

Printed and bound in China

10 9 8 7 6 5 4 3 2 1

Both metric and imperial measurements are given for the recipes.
Use one set of measures only, not a mixture of both.

Ovens should be preheated to the specified temperature. If using a
fan-assisted oven, follow the manufacturer's instructions for adjusting
the time and temperature. Grills should also be preheated.

This books includes dishes made with nuts and nut derivatives.
It is advisable for those with known allergic reactions to nuts and nut
derivatives and those who may be potentially vulnerable to these
allergies, such as pregnant and nursing mothers, invalids, the elderly,
babies and children, to avoid dishes made with nuts and nut oils.
It is also prudent to check the labels of preprepared ingredients for
the possible inclusion of nut derivatives.

The Department of Health advises that eggs should not be consumed
raw. This book contains some dishes made with raw or lightly cooked
eggs. It is prudent for more vulnerable people such as pregnant and
nursing mothers, invalids, the elderly, babies and young children to
avoid uncooked or lightly cooked dishes made with eggs.

Meat and poultry should be cooked thoroughly. To test if poultry is
cooked, pierce the flesh through the thickest part with a skewer or fork
– the juices should run clear, never pink or red.

Contents

Introduction

Chinese cuisine reflects the long history and vast geographic and climatic diversity of China itself. From Beijing (Peking) in the very cold north to Guangzhou (Canton) in the hot subtropical south, and from cosmopolitan Shanghai and the eastern provinces to the exotic regions bordering Tibet, it displays distinctive variations, but all are based on the shared central themes of its venerable cooking tradition.

Highly nutritious, the Chinese diet relies heavily on fresh and preserved vegetables, a staple grain such as rice, and fish and seafood with relatively little meat. Techniques allow for efficient cooking, whether fast or slow, that preserves nutrients, flavours and textures. The famous yin and yang philosophy that informs Chinese cuisine may be seen as no more than an emphasis on certain combinations of foods and ingredients, prepared in a certain way. All Chinese styles share the common goal of the harmonious blending of natural tastes, textures, colours and aromas, enhanced but never obscured by sauces and dips.

The recipes in this book offer a representative sample of authentic Chinese cuisine, and I have sought to include those that illustrate both the central themes of Chinese cookery and the various regional variations played on those themes. You will find them all delectable.

Ingredients

All the ingredients used in this book can now be obtained in ordinary supermarkets, with perhaps just one or two items to be found in Chinese or Asian grocers.

Black beans These small, black fermented soya beans have a distinctive, slightly salty taste and a rich smell, and are used as a seasoning, often in conjunction with garlic or fresh root ginger. They will keep indefinitely in the refrigerator.

Chinese long beans There are two varieties: pale green and thinner dark green. You will usually find them sold in looped bunches, and there is no need to trim them. They have a crunchy taste and texture like green beans but cook faster.

Dried citrus peel This is sold in Chinese or Asian grocery stores.

7

Five-spice powder This is a mixture of star anise, Sichuan peppercorns, fennel, cloves and cinnamon.

Lily buds These provide texture as well as an earthy taste to any dish. Store them in a jar in a dry place. Soak before use – see recipe instructions.

Mushrooms, Chinese dried Black or brown in colour, these add a particular flavour and aroma to dishes. Keep them in an airtight jar in a cool, dry place. Soak before use – see recipe instructions.

Mushrooms, Chinese dried cloud ear These puff up to look like clouds when soaked (see recipe instructions) and are valued for their crunchy texture.

Mushrooms, Chinese dried wood ear (tree ear) These are the larger variety of the above fungi. Once soaked, they will swell up to four or five times their size.

Mooli (Chinese white radish) Long, white and carrot-like in shape, mooli absorbs the flavours of the food it is cooked with yet retains its distinctive radish taste and texture. They are always peeled.

Shaoxing rice wine I believe the finest of the many varieties of rice wine to be from Shaoxing in Zhejiang Province in eastern China. It is used not only for cooking but also in marinades and for sauces. It should be kept tightly corked at room temperature.

Yellow bean sauce (whole and ground) This thick, spicy, aromatic sauce is made with yellow beans, flour and salt, fermented together. Correctly blended, it is quite salty but provides a distinctive flavour to sauces. There are two forms: whole beans in a thick sauce and mashed or puréed beans.

Chilli bean sauce This is a thick, dark, hot and spicy sauce or paste made from soya beans, chillies and other seasonings, and widely used in western China.

Chilli sauce A bright red, hot sauce made from chillies, vinegar, sugar and salt, most often used as a dipping sauce.

Hoisin sauce Widely used in southern China, this is a thick, dark, brownish-red sauce made from soya beans, vinegar, sugar, spices and other flavourings, and is sweet and slightly spicy.

Oyster sauce This is an essential ingredient of Cantonese cuisine, but is also used in other regions. Thick and brown, it is made from a concentrate of oysters cooked in soy sauce, seasonings and brine. It has a rich, savoury flavour without being fishy and is used not only in cooking but as a condiment, diluted with a little oil. The expensive kinds are worth their extra cost.

Sesame paste This rich, thick, creamy brown paste is made from toasted sesame seeds and is used in both hot and cold dishes. If the paste has separated in the jar, empty the contents into a food processor or blender and blend well.

Sichuan peppercorns These are reddish-brown in colour with a strong pungent odour that distinguishes them from the hotter black peppercorns. Their taste is sharp and mildly spicy, and while they can be ground in a conventional peppermill, they should be roasted before they are ground to bring out their full flavour.

Sichuan preserved vegetables This is one of the most popular preserved vegetables in China, a specialty of Sichuan Province. It is sold in cans in Chinese grocers and gives a pleasantly crunchy texture and spicy taste to dishes. Rinse before use.

Sugar I particularly like to use rock sugar, which is richer and has a more subtle flavour than refined granulated sugar and also gives a good lustre or glaze to braised dishes and sauces. Buy it in Chinese markets, but if you cannot find it, use plain sugar or amber coffee sugar crystals instead.

Tofu (beancurd) Tofu is highly nutritious, rich in protein and has a distinctive smooth texture but a bland taste. It is usually sold in two forms: as small, firm blocks or a soft, custard-like (silken) variety. But it is also available in several dried forms and in a fermented version. Silken tofu is used for soups and other dishes, while firm tofu is used for stir-frying, braising and deep-frying.

Vinegar, white rice This is clear and mild in flavour, and has a faint taste of glutinous rice. It is used for sweet and sour dishes.

Vinegar, black rice This is very dark in colour with a rich but mild taste. It is used for braised dishes, noodles and sauces.

Choosing a wok

The shape of the wok allows heat to spread evenly over its surface, thus making for rapid cooking, which is fundamental to stir-frying. When used for deep-frying, because its base is smaller a wok requires less cooking oil while still providing necessary depth.

I have found that the most appropriate wok for a Western-type hob is one with a long wooden handle. The wok should be about 30–36 cm (12–14 inches) in diameter with deep sides and a slightly flattened bottom. Select one that has heft to it, and, if possible, made of carbon steel rather than of light stainless steel or aluminium, which tend to scorch. A lid, usually aluminium, normally comes with the wok, but can be purchased separately. A long-handled metal spatula shaped rather like a small shovel is ideal for scooping and tossing food in a wok.

Seasoning and cleaning

Before its first use, scrub your wok with kitchen cleanser and water to remove as much of the machine oil applied to the surface by the manufacturer as possible. Dry the wok and place it over a low heat. Add 2 tablespoons cooking oil and rub over the inside with kitchen paper until lightly coated. Heat the wok slowly for

10–15 minutes and then wipe it thoroughly with clean kitchen paper. Repeat coating, heating and wiping until the paper comes out clean. Once seasoned, your wok will darken with use. Wash a seasoned wok in water without detergent and dry it thoroughly to prevent rusting.

Steamers and steaming rack

Basket-like bamboo steamers come in several sizes; the 25 cm (10 inch) size is the most suitable for home use. It is placed on top of a saucepan or over a wok of boiling water. Clean damp muslin is sometimes laid over the open slats under the food to prevent the steam escaping. Before using for the first time, wash and steam it empty for about 5 minutes. Alternatively, use any kind of wide metal steamer.

If using your wok or a large saucepan as a steamer, you will need a wooden or metal rack or trivet to stand above the water level and support the plate of food to be steamed. Some woks are sold with a round metal stand, but you can buy triangular wooden stands or round metal stands for this purpose.

Choosing a cleaver

No self-respecting Chinese cook would be seen with a knife instead of a cleaver. These heavy choppers are used for all kinds of cutting ranging from fine shredding to chopping up bones. Of course, you can prepare Chinese food using good sharp knives, but if you decide to buy a cleaver, you will be surprised at how easy it is to use. Choose a good-quality, medium-sized, all-purpose, stainless steel one.

Soups

Corn and Crab Soup
Su Mi Rou Tang

SERVES: 4

1.2 litres (2 pints) chicken stock

500 g (1 lb) fresh corn cobs, kernels removed, or 250 g (8 oz) frozen sweetcorn kernels

1 teaspoon peeled and finely chopped fresh root ginger

2 teaspoons Shaoxing rice wine or dry sherry

1 teaspoon salt

1½ teaspoons sugar

175 g (6 oz) cooked crabmeat (white meat only)

1 egg white, beaten

½ teaspoon sesame oil

freshly ground white pepper

chopped spring onions, to garnish

A popular soup in southern China, where corn, a relatively recent addition to the repertory of Chinese cookery, is much in use today. Its sweetness goes well with crabmeat.

1 Put the stock into a medium-sized saucepan and bring it to a simmer. Add the corn and ginger and cook for 2 minutes over a low heat. Add the rice wine or sherry, ½ teaspoon of the salt, ½ teaspoon of the sugar and the crabmeat and continue to simmer for 2 minutes.

2 Combine the egg white with the sesame oil and the remaining salt. Add the egg white mixture to the stock in a very slow, thin and steady stream. Using a chopstick or fork, pull the egg white slowly into strands. Add the remaining sugar and pepper to taste. Garnish with chopped spring onions and serve at once.

Basic Clear Chicken Stock or Soup
Ching Tang

MAKES:
4 LITRES
(7 PINTS)

1.25 kg (2½ lb) chicken pieces and bones, preferably from a stewing (old) hen, such as backs, feet, wings, etc. – use 50% bones and 50% meat

2 litres (3½ pints) cold water

4 x 5 cm (2 inch) pieces of fresh root ginger

4 spring onions

6 whole garlic cloves

2 teaspoons Sichuan peppercorns

2 teaspoons black peppercorns

½ teaspoon salt

Good stock is especially essential to Chinese cooking. Because of its lightness, flavour and versatility, chicken stock should be considered a staple like salt, cooking oil or soy sauce.

1 Put the chicken pieces and bones into a very large, tall, heavy pot, cover them with the cold water and bring it to a simmer. Meanwhile, peel the ginger and remove the green tops of the spring onions. Lightly crush the garlic cloves leaving the skins on. To roast the Sichuan peppercorns, heat a wok or frying pan to a medium heat, add the peppercorns and stir-fry them for about 5 minutes until they brown slightly and start to smoke. Leave them to cool. (You can roast up to 125 g (4 oz) and store in a well-sealed container for later use.)

2 Using a large, flat spoon, gently skim off the scum as it rises from the bones. Watch the heat, as the stock should *never* boil, otherwise it will become cloudy and heavy. Keep skimming until the stock looks clear. This can take 20–40 minutes. Do not stir or disturb the stock.

3 Reduce the heat to a low simmer. Add the ginger, spring onions, garlic cloves, Sichuan and black peppercorns and salt. Simmer the stock on a very low heat for 4 hours, skimming any fat or scum off the top at least twice during this time. The stock should be rich and full-bodied, which is why it needs to be simmered for such a long time. This way the stock (and any soup you make with it) will have plenty of taste.

4 Strain the stock through several layers of dampened muslin or a very fine sieve, and then let it cool. Remove any fat that has risen to the top. It is now ready to be used or transferred to containers and frozen for future use.

Cabbage and Pork Soup
Bai Cai Tang

SERVES: 4

1.2 litres (2 pints) chicken stock

175 g (6 oz) lean pork, shredded

4 teaspoons light soy sauce

2 teaspoons Shaoxing rice wine or dry sherry

½ teaspoon sesame oil

½ teaspoon cornflour

1 tablespoon groundnut or vegetable oil

375 g (12 oz) Chinese leaves, shredded widthways

1 teaspoon dark soy sauce

salt and freshly ground black pepper

chopped spring onions, to garnish

Chinese leaves (Peking cabbage) with its tightly packed, firm, crinkled leaves has a sweet taste and pleasing texture, making it a popular ingredient in China for soups.

1 Put the stock into a medium-sized saucepan and bring it to a simmer. Combine the pork with half the light soy sauce, half the rice wine or sherry, the sesame oil and the cornflour.

2 Heat a wok until it is hot, then add the groundnut or vegetable oil. When the oil is hot and slightly smoking, add the pork and stir-fry for 1 minute. Remove from the heat and set aside.

3 Add the Chinese leaves, the remaining rice wine or sherry and light soy sauce and the dark soy sauce to the simmering stock and simmer for another 5 minutes. Add the pork to the stock and simmer for a further minute. Season to taste with salt and pepper.

4 Transfer to individual soup bowls or a large soup tureen. Garnish with chopped spring onions and serve at once.

Beancurd Spinach Soup
Dou Fou Bo Cai Tang

SERVES: 4

500 g (1 lb) fresh
  spinach

285 g (9½ oz) packet
  silken (soft) tofu
  (beancurd)

1.2 litres (2 pints)
  chicken stock

1 tablespoon Shaoxing
  rice wine or dry
  sherry

1 tablespoon light soy
  sauce

1 teaspoon sugar

1 teaspoon sesame oil

1 teaspoon dark soy
  sauce

salt and freshly ground
  black pepper

chopped spring onions,
  to garnish

Subtly flavoured and textured as well as colourful, this soup contrasts bright green spinach with healthy white tofu (beancurd). This makes a perfect starter for any meal.

1 Remove the stems from the spinach, pick over the leaves and wash them well. Leave them to drain in a colander. Gently cut the tofu into 1 cm (½ inch) cubes and drain on kitchen paper for 10 minutes.

2 Put the stock into a medium-sized saucepan and bring it to a simmer. Add the tofu and simmer for 2 minutes.

3 Add the rest of the ingredients except the spinach and simmer for another 10 minutes. The tofu will swell, taking on the flavour of the soup. Finally, add the spinach leaves and cook for 2 minutes. Garnish with chopped spring onions and serve in individual bowls or a soup tureen.

Minced Beef and Rice Noodles in Soup
Mian Zhi Niu Rou Wo Mi

SERVES: 4

250 g (8 oz) dried rice
  noodles, round or flat

375 g (12 oz) minced
  beef

1½ tablespoons
  groundnut or
  vegetable oil

1½ tablespoons finely
  chopped garlic

2 tablespoons finely
  chopped spring
  onions, white
  part only

2 teaspoons peeled and
  finely chopped fresh
  root ginger

1.2 litres (2 pints)
  chicken stock

3 tablespoons light soy
  sauce

salt

chopped spring onions,
  to garnish

MARINADE

2 teaspoons Shaoxing
  rice wine or dry
  sherry

1 teaspoon dark soy
  sauce

2 teaspoons light soy
  sauce

2 teaspoons sugar

freshly ground black
  pepper, to taste

2 teaspoons sesame oil

Rice noodles are as delicious in soup as they are stir-fried. In this case, much of the broth is soaked up by them, providing a substantial, lip-smacking snack.

1 Soak the noodles in warm water for 15 minutes or until they are soft. Drain well in a colander and set aside.

2 Put the beef and all the marinade ingredients into a bowl and mix well.

3 Heat a wok until it is hot, then add the oil. When the oil is hot and slightly smoking, add the garlic, spring onion and ginger and stir-fry for 30 seconds. Then add the beef, stir well to break up all the pieces and continue to stir-fry for 5 minutes. Drain the meat well in a colander.

4 Bring the stock to a simmer in a medium-sized saucepan, add the rice noodles, soy sauce and salt to taste and cook for 2 minutes. Then add the beef and simmer together for 5 minutes. Garnish with chopped spring onions and serve in individual bowls or a soup tureen.

Egg Flower Tomato Soup
Dan Hua Fangie Tang

SERVES: 4

2 small eggs, beaten

1 teaspoon sesame oil

½ teaspoon salt

1.2 litres (2 pints) chicken stock

250 g (8 oz) fresh or canned tomatoes, peeled, deseeded and chopped

1 teaspoon peeled and finely chopped fresh root ginger

1 teaspoon Shaoxing rice wine or dry sherry

2 teaspoons light soy sauce

salt and freshly ground black pepper

chopped spring onions, to garnish

This light soup capitalizes on the tomato's brilliant colour and distinctive flavour. The 'egg flowers' are made by stretching the egg strands as you pour them slowly into the soup.

1 Combine the beaten eggs, sesame oil and salt in a small bowl.

2 Put the stock into a medium-sized saucepan and bring it to a simmer. Add the tomatoes and ginger and cook for 2 minutes over a low heat.

3 Add the rice wine or sherry and soy sauce to the simmering stock. Then add the egg mixture in a very slow, thin and steady stream. Using a chopstick or fork, pull the egg slowly into strands. Season to taste with salt and pepper. Garnish with chopped spring onions and serve at once.

Asparagus Minced Chicken Soup
Ji Yung Lu Sun Tang

SERVES: 2 – 4

1.2 litres (2 pints)
chicken stock

250 g (8 oz) fresh
asparagus

250 g (8 oz) boneless,
skinless chicken
breasts

1 egg white

1 teaspoon sesame oil

½ teaspoon salt

2 teaspoons Shaoxing
rice wine or dry
sherry

2 teaspoons light soy
sauce

1 teaspoon salt

freshly ground black
pepper

chopped spring onions,
to garnish

Although asparagus is a relative newcomer among Chinese vegetables, it is now enjoyed throughout China. It is paired with chicken mixed with egg white in this delicately flavoured soup.

1 Put the stock into a medium-sized saucepan and bring it to a simmer. Cut the asparagus at a slight diagonal into 2.5 cm (1 inch) pieces.

2 Cut the chicken breasts into small pieces. Put them with the egg white, sesame oil and salt into a food processor or blender and blend until smooth. Transfer to a small bowl, cover with clingfilm and chill in the refrigerator for 5 minutes.

3 Add the asparagus, rice wine or sherry and soy sauce to the simmering stock. Cook for 3 minutes or until the asparagus is cooked. Remove the pan from the heat. Add the chicken mixture, stirring vigorously to break up any large lumps. Return to the heat and simmer for another minute. Garnish with chopped spring onions and serve at once.

Wonton Soup
Huntun Tang

SERVES: 4

250 g (8 oz) wonton skins

1.2 litres (2 pints) chicken stock

salt

chopped spring onions, to garnish

FILLING

250 g (8 oz) raw peeled prawns, deveined and chopped or coarsely minced

250 g (8 oz) minced pork

½ teaspoon freshly ground white pepper

2 tablespoons light soy sauce

2 tablespoons finely chopped spring onions

2 teaspoons Shaoxing rice wine or dry sherry

1 teaspoon sugar

1 teaspoon sesame oil

1 egg white, lightly beaten

You can find many versions of this famous, satisfying soup in food stalls and street restaurants throughout China. My favourite is this one from the south.

1 To make the filling, put the prawns and pork into a large bowl, add 1 teaspoon salt and the pepper and mix well, either by kneading with your hands or by stirring with a wooden spoon. Then add all the other filling ingredients and stir them well into the prawn and pork mixture. Cover the bowl with clingfilm and chill in the refrigerator for at least 20 minutes.

2 When you are ready to stuff the wontons, place 1 tablespoon of the filling in the centre of the first wonton skin. Dampen the edges with a little water and bring up the sides of the skin around the filling. Pinch the edges together at the top so that the wonton is sealed – it should look like a small filled bag.

3 When the wontons are ready, bring the stock to a simmer in a large saucepan. In a separate large saucepan, bring salted water to the boil, add the wontons and poach for 1 minute or until they float to the surface. Remove them immediately and transfer them to the stock. (This procedure will result in a cleaner-tasting broth.) Continue to simmer them in the stock for 2 minutes. Transfer to individual bowls or a large soup tureen, garnish with chopped spring onions and serve immediately

Hot and Sour Soup
Suan La Tang

SERVES: 4

15 g (½ oz) Chinese dried wood ear (tree ear) mushrooms

25 g (1 oz) Chinese dried mushrooms

1.2 litres (2 pints) chicken stock

2 teaspoons salt

125 g (4 oz) lean boneless pork, finely shredded

2 eggs, beaten with a pinch of salt

2 teaspoons sesame oil

250 g (8 oz) firm tofu (beancurd), drained and shredded

1½ tablespoons light soy sauce

1 tablespoon dark soy sauce

1 teaspoon white pepper

6 tablespoons white rice wine vinegar

2 teaspoons sesame oil

1 tablespoon chilli oil

2 tablespoons finely chopped coriander

MARINADE

1 teaspoon light soy sauce

1 teaspoon Shaoxing rice wine or dry sherry

½ teaspoon sesame oil

½ teaspoon cornflour

pinch of salt

pinch of sugar

This hearty soup offers a variety of textures and contrasting flavours, and makes an engaging alternative to Western-style soups. It is perfect for an autumn or winter evening.

1 Soak the wood ear (tree ear) mushrooms in warm water for 20–30 minutes and the Chinese dried mushrooms for 20 minutes until soft. Drain the latter, squeeze out any excess liquid and remove and discard the stems, then finely shred. Rinse the wood ear mushrooms well, remove and discard the stems, then finely shred.

2 Bring the stock to a simmer in a large saucepan and add the salt.

3 Put the pork and all the marinade ingredients into a bowl and mix well. In a small bowl, combine the beaten eggs with the sesame oil.

4 Stir the pork mixture into the stock and simmer for 1 minute. Then add the mushrooms and tofu and continue to simmer for 2 minutes. Add the egg mixture in a very slow, thin and steady stream. Using a chopstick or fork, pull the egg slowly into strands.

5 Remove the soup from the heat and stir in the soy sauces, pepper and vinegar. Give the soup a good stir, then finally add the sesame oil, chilli oil and fresh coriander and stir. Ladle into individual bowls or a large soup tureen and serve at once.

Chinese Cabbage Soup
Qing Tang Bai Cai Tang

SERVES: 4

1.2 litres (2 pints) chicken stock, or use vegetable stock or water for a vegetarian version

500 g (1 lb) Chinese leaves, shredded widthways

125 g (4 oz) Sichuan preserved vegetables, rinsed thoroughly and finely chopped

1 tablespoon light soy sauce

2 teaspoons dark soy sauce

2 tablespoons Shaoxing rice wine or dry sherry

2 teaspoons sugar

2 teaspoons sesame oil

salt and freshly ground black pepper

chopped spring onions, to garnish

This light, refreshing clear soup is consumed as a beverage throughout the meal. The Chinese leaves add a touch of sweetness, while the preserved vegetables give it a bite.

1 Put the stock into a medium-sized saucepan and bring it to a simmer. Add the Chinese leaves and preserved vegetables and simmer for 3 minutes. Then add the soy sauces, rice wine or sherry and sugar and simmer for 5 minutes.

2 Season to taste with salt and pepper and stir in the sesame oil. Transfer to individual soup bowls or a large soup tureen, garnish with chopped spring onions and serve at once.

Sweet Walnut Cream
He Tao Lao

SERVES: 4

175 g (6 oz) shelled walnuts

450 ml (¾ pint) water

600 ml (1 pint) semi-skimmed milk

150 g (5 oz) sugar

Some of China's most appealing desserts are in the form of light, sweet, warm soups. This is an easy, if uncommon, one that will quickly become a favourite.

1 Rinse the walnuts well in warm water and drain. Put on a baking sheet and bake in a preheated oven, 180°C (350°F), Gas Mark 4, for 15 minutes or until they are light brown and crisp. Remove from the oven and leave to cool.

2 Put the walnuts and water into a blender and blend until the walnuts are reduced to a fine purée, adding more water if necessary. Strain the mixture through a fine sieve.

3 Combine the walnut purée and milk in a medium-sized saucepan and simmer for 1 minute. Beat in the sugar and simmer for 2 minutes. Serve in individual bowls or in a large soup tureen.

Almond Cream
Xien Ren Lu

SERVES: 4

250 g (8 oz) almond paste or marzipan

250 ml (8 fl oz) semi-skimmed milk

450 ml (¾ pint) water

2 teaspoons vanilla extract

Using a food processor or blender for grinding almonds can make them taste bitter. But to save grinding by hand, use ready-made almond paste for this fragrant sweet dessert.

1 Break up the almond paste with your fingers. Combine it with the milk, water and vanilla extract in a medium-sized saucepan and simmer for 15 minutes.

2 Strain the mixture through a fine sieve. Serve in individual soup bowls or a large soup tureen. It can be served either hot or cold.

Meat

Meat-filled Omelette
Dan Jia

This hearty dish is full of rich flavours and aromas that typify the country cuisine of Sichuan. The omelette wrapping absorbs the juices from both the filling and sauce.

SERVES: 4

OMELETTE
WRAPPERS

3 large eggs, beaten

3 tablespoons plain
flour

1 tablespoon sesame oil

pinch of salt

groundnut or vegetable
oil, for greasing

FILLING

250 g (8 oz) minced pork

1 tablespoon peeled and
finely chopped fresh
root ginger

3 tablespoons finely
chopped spring
onions

1 tablespoon light soy
sauce

2 tablespoons Shaoxing
rice wine or dry
sherry

2 teaspoons sesame oil

1 egg white, beaten

2 teaspoons cornflour

1 teaspoon roasted
ground Sichuan
peppercorns

½ teaspoon salt

½ teaspoon freshly
ground black pepper

beaten egg, for sealing

1 For the omelette wrappers, put the beaten eggs, flour, sesame oil and salt into a blender and blend until it is a smooth batter with *no* lumps. Strain through a fine sieve.

2 Heat a wok over medium heat until it is hot, then grease the surface with groundnut or vegetable oil on kitchen paper. Put 2 tablespoons of the egg batter in the wok and tilt the wok in all directions to coat the bottom. When the batter has set, carefully peel it off and lay it on a plate. Repeat the process until you have used up all the batter.

3 Mix all the filling ingredients, except the beaten egg for sealing, together in a bowl. Put about 2 tablespoons of the filling in the centre of each omelette. Moisten the edges of each omelette with the beaten egg and fold over one half to seal, to make half-moon-shaped dumplings. Any leftover filling can be used in the sauce.

4 For the sauce, heat a wok over a high heat until it is hot, then add the groundnut or vegetable oil. When the oil is hot and slightly smoking, add the spring onions and garlic and stir-fry for 20 seconds, then add the lily buds and cloud ear mushrooms and stir-fry for 1 minute. Add the rest of the sauce ingredients except the sesame oil. Bring the sauce to the boil and add the dumplings to the sauce. Reduce the heat to very low, cover and simmer for 15 minutes, then add the sesame oil.

5 Turn the dish onto a platter and serve at once, with rice and vegetables for a robust winter meal.

SAUCE

- 1½ tablespoons groundnut or vegetable oil
- 3 tablespoons finely shredded spring onions
- 4 garlic cloves, thinly sliced
- 25 g (1 oz) dried lily buds, soaked in hot water for 30 minutes or until soft, ends removed
- 15 g (½ oz) Chinese dried cloud ear mushrooms, soaked in hot water for 20–30 minutes, rinsed and stems removed
- 2 tablespoons Shaoxing rice wine or dry sherry
- 1 tablespoon light soy sauce
- 1 tablespoon dark soy sauce
- 2 teaspoons sugar
- 1 teaspoon roasted ground Sichuan peppercorns
- 1 teaspoon salt
- 300 ml (½ pint) chicken stock
- 2 teaspoons sesame oil

Minced Beef with Scrambled Eggs
Hua Dan Niu Rou

SERVES: 2 – 4

250 g (8 oz) minced beef

1 tablespoon groundnut or vegetable oil, plus 1½ tablespoons

6 eggs, beaten

2 teaspoons sesame oil

½ teaspoon salt

pinch of freshly ground black pepper

4 tablespoons finely chopped spring onions, plus extra to garnish

MARINADE

2 teaspoons light soy sauce

2 teaspoons Shaoxing rice wine or dry sherry

2 teaspoons sesame oil

1 teaspoon sugar

pinch of salt

freshly ground black pepper

Eggs are commonly found in many home-cooked dishes in China. Here, minced beef is marinated, stir-fried and then mixed with stir-fried eggs for a quick, inexpensive meal.

1 Combine the beef with all the marinade ingredients and pepper to taste in a bowl.

2 Heat a wok until it is hot, then add the 1 tablespoon groundnut or vegetable oil. When the oil is hot and slightly smoking, add the beef mixture and stir-fry for 2 minutes. Remove and drain well in a colander.

3 Combine the beaten eggs with the sesame oil, salt, pepper and spring onions in a bowl.

4 Wipe the wok clean and reheat. When the wok is hot, add the remaining 1½ tablespoons groundnut or vegetable oil, and when the oil begins to slightly smoke, swirl it around the entire side of the wok. Add the egg mixture and stir-fry over a high heat, folding and lifting it, until the egg begins to set slightly. Return the beef to the wok and continue to stir-fry for another minute to finish cooking the eggs and to reheat the beef.

5 Turn the mixture onto a platter, garnish with chopped spring onions and serve at once, with plain rice and stir-fried vegetables.

Stir-fried Pork with Bean Sprouts
Yin Ya Rou Si

SERVES: 4

500 g (1 lb) boneless
  lean pork, shredded

1½ tablespoons
  groundnut or
  vegetable oil

1 tablespoon finely
  chopped garlic

4 spring onions, finely
  shredded

1 red pepper, cored,
  deseeded and finely
  shredded

250 g (8 oz) fresh bean
  sprouts

1 teaspoon salt

1 teaspoon sugar

1 tablespoon light soy
  sauce

2 teaspoons dark soy
  sauce

1 tablespoon Shaoxing
  rice wine or dry
  sherry

1½ teaspoons sesame
  oil

salt and freshly ground
  black pepper

MARINADE

1 tablespoon Shaoxing
  rice wine or dry
  sherry

1 tablespoon light soy
  sauce

1 teaspoon sesame oil

1 teaspoon cornflour

At dinnertime in Chinese homes there is almost always at least one pork dish. In this quick and easy home-style recipe it is combined with refreshing bean sprouts.

1 Combine the pork with all the marinade ingredients in a bowl.

2 Heat a wok over a high heat until it is hot, then add the groundnut or vegetable oil. When the oil is hot and slightly smoking, add the pork mixture and stir-fry for 1 minute. Remove the pork with a slotted spoon and set aside in a bowl.

3 Quickly add the garlic to the wok and stir-fry for 10 seconds, then add the spring onions, red pepper and bean sprouts and stir-fry for 10 seconds. Add the salt, sugar, soy sauces and rice wine or sherry and cook for 2 minutes.

4 Return the pork to the wok and stir-fry, mixing well, for another minute. Add the sesame oil and give the mixture another minute to cook or until the pork is heated through. Season to taste with salt and pepper and serve at once, with plain rice and a vegetable dish.

Stir-fried Eggs with Meats and Vegetables
Liu Huang Cai

SERVES: 4

250 g (8 oz) minced pork

1 tablespoon groundnut or vegetable oil, plus 1½ tablespoons

6 eggs, beaten

2 teaspoons sesame oil

½ teaspoon salt

pinch of freshly ground black pepper

3 tablespoons finely chopped spring onions

1 small onion, thinly sliced

125 g (4 oz) frozen peas

50 g (2 oz) cooked ham, chopped

2 tablespoons oyster sauce

chopped spring onions, to garnish

MARINADE

2 teaspoons light soy sauce

2 teaspoons Shaoxing rice wine or dry sherry

2 teaspoons sesame oil

1 teaspoon sugar

pinch of salt

A variation of the 'fu-yung' so well known in takeaways, this is a satisfying dish that is easy to make, and one typically found in many Chinese homes.

1 Combine the pork with the all the marinade ingredients in a bowl.

2 Heat a wok until it is hot, then add the 1 tablespoon groundnut or vegetable oil. When the oil is hot and slightly smoking, add the pork mixture and stir-fry for 2 minutes. Remove and drain well in a colander.

3 Combine the beaten eggs with the sesame oil, salt, pepper and spring onions in a bowl.

4 Wipe the wok clean and reheat. When the wok is hot, add the 1½ tablespoons groundnut or vegetable oil, and when the oil begins to slightly smoke, swirl the oil around the entire side of the wok. Add the onion, peas and ham and stir-fry for 3 minutes. Then add the egg mixture and stir-fry over a high heat, folding and lifting it, until the egg begins to set slightly. Return the pork to the wok and continue to stir-fry for another minute to finish cooking the eggs and to reheat the pork.

5 Turn the mixture onto a platter and add the oyster sauce. Garnish with chopped spring onions and serve at once, with rice and a vegetable dish for a wholesome meal.

Sweet and Sour Pork Spareribs
Kun Shao Pai Gu

375 g (12 oz) meaty pork spareribs

cornflour, for dusting

1 egg, beaten

600 ml (1 pint) groundnut oil, plus 1½ tablespoons

2 tablespoons finely chopped garlic

1 small onion, thinly sliced

125 g (4 oz) frozen peas

325 g (11 oz) canned lychees, drained

MARINADE

2 teaspoons light soy sauce

2 teaspoons Shaoxing rice wine or dry sherry

1 teaspoon salt

½ teaspoon freshly ground black pepper

SAUCE

150 ml (¼ pint) chicken stock

1 tablespoon light soy sauce

1 teaspoon salt

5 tablespoons white rice vinegar

3 tablespoons tomato purée or ketchup

3 tablespoons sugar

2 teaspoons cornflour, blended with 1 tablespoon water to a smooth paste

This is perhaps the most famous Chinese dish outside China. Properly made, as here, there is a fine balance between the sweet and sour flavours that merits its popularity.

1 Cut the pork into 2.5 cm (1 inch) pieces and put in a bowl with all the marinade ingredients and mix well. Cover with clingfilm and leave to marinate in a cool place for 30 minutes.

2 Put the marinated pork pieces on a baking sheet. Sprinkle cornflour evenly over each piece of pork and shake off any excess. Baste the pork with the beaten egg and again coat each side of the pork with cornflour, shaking off any excess.

3 Heat a wok over a high heat until it is hot, then add the 600 ml (1 pint) oil. When the oil is slightly smoking, add the pork and deep-fry for 5–7 minutes or until golden brown. You will need to do this in at least 2 batches. Discard the oil and wipe the wok clean with kitchen paper.

4 Reheat the wok over a high heat until it is hot, then add the remaining 1½ tablespoons oil. When the oil is hot and slightly smoking, add the garlic and onion and stir-fry for 20 seconds. Then add the peas and continue to stir-fry for 2 minutes. Add the lychees and all the sauce ingredients except the cornflour paste. Bring the mixture to the boil, add the cornflour paste and cook until thickened.

5 Reduce the heat to a simmer, return the pork to the wok and cook for 3 minutes or until heated through. Turn onto a deep platter and serve at once.

Stir-fried Ginger Beef
Xin Jiang Chao Niu Rou

SERVES: 4

500 g (1 lb) lean fillet or sirloin steak

3 tablespoons groundnut or vegetable oil

8 thin slices of fresh root ginger, peeled and finely shredded

2 garlic cloves, thinly sliced

2 tablespoons chicken stock

2 teaspoons sesame oil

1 tablespoon oyster sauce

chopped spring onions, to garnish

MARINADE

2 teaspoons light soy sauce

1 tablespoon Shaoxing rice wine or dry sherry

2 teaspoons sesame oil

¼ teaspoon salt

pinch of sugar

1 tablespoon cornflour

I like using fillet steak not only for its tenderness but also because it has little fat and cooks quickly. The ginger adds a subtle and fragrant spiciness.

1 Cut the beef into slices about 3 cm (1¼ inches) long and 5 mm (¼ inch) thick. Put the beef into a bowl, add all the marinade ingredients and mix well.

2 Heat a wok over a high heat until it is hot, then add the groundnut or vegetable oil. When the oil is very hot and begins to smoke, add the beef. Let the meat brown for 1 minute, then carefully stir-fry for another minute. Drain the beef in a colander, leaving 1 tablespoon oil in the wok.

3 Quickly reheat the wok and the oil. When it is hot, add the ginger and garlic and stir-fry for 20 seconds over a medium heat. Then add the stock, give the mixture a stir and return the meat to the wok and stir to mix well. Add the sesame oil and oyster sauce and give the mixture several stirs to mix well.

4 Turn onto a platter, garnish with chopped spring onions and serve at once, with fried or plain rice and a vegetable or fish dish.

Stewed Pork Spareribs (Shandong)
Ba Zi Rou

SERVES: 4

500 g (1 lb) meaty pork
  spareribs

2 tablespoons
  groundnut or
  vegetable oil

8 garlic cloves, crushed

8 slices of fresh root
  ginger, peeled and
  finely chopped

4 spring onions, cut into
  8 cm (3¼ inch) pieces

2 teaspoons five-spice
  powder

3 tablespoons rock or
  granulated sugar

2 tablespoons dark soy
  sauce

150 ml (¼ pint) black
  rice vinegar

150 ml (¼ pint) Shaoxing
  rice wine or dry
  sherry

150 ml (¼ pint) chicken
  stock

The spareribs are first blanched to remove excess fat, briefly stir-fried to give them colour and then braised in a piquant sauce to make them succulent and tender.

1 Cut the spareribs into 5 cm (2 inch) pieces. Blanch them in salted boiling water for 10 minutes. Drain well and discard the water.

2 Heat a wok over a high heat until it is hot, then add the oil. When the oil is hot and slightly smoking, add the garlic, ginger and spring onions and stir-fry for 1 minute. Then add the spareribs and stir-fry for 4 minutes or until they are lightly browned.

3 Add the rest of the ingredients and bring the mixture to the boil. Transfer the contents to a flameproof casserole, cover and simmer for 40 minutes or until the meat is very tender. Serve with rice.

Spicy Stir-fried Hunan Beef
Sa Cha Niu Nan

SERVES: 4

500 g (1 lb) lean fillet or
sirloin steak

3 tablespoons
groundnut or
vegetable oil

2 tablespoons black
beans, coarsely
chopped

2 tablespoons finely
chopped garlic

1 tablespoon peeled and
finely chopped fresh
root ginger

2 large fresh red
chillies, deseeded and
finely shredded

2 large fresh green
chillies, deseeded and
finely shredded

3 tablespoons chicken
stock

1½ tablespoons
Shaoxing rice wine or
dry sherry

1 tablespoon light soy
sauce

2 teaspoons sugar

2 teaspoons sesame oil

MARINADE

2 teaspoons light soy
sauce

1 tablespoon Shaoxing
rice wine or dry
sherry

2 teaspoons sesame oil

2 teaspoons salt

2 teaspoons cornflour

As is usual when beef is served in Chinese cuisine, this dish utilizes strong, pungent and aromatic ingredients to enhance the taste and colour of the meat.

1 Cut the beef into slices about 3 cm (1¼ inches) long and 5 mm (¼ inch) thick. Stack up the slices and then finely shred the meat. Put the beef into a bowl, add all the marinade ingredients and mix well.

2 Heat a wok over a high heat until it is hot, then add the groundnut or vegetable oil. When the oil is very hot and begins to smoke, add the beef. Let the meat brown for 1 minute, then carefully stir-fry for another minute. Drain the beef in a colander, leaving 1 tablespoon oil in the wok.

3 Quickly reheat the wok and the oil. When it is hot, add the black beans, garlic and ginger and stir-fry for 20 seconds over a medium heat. Add the chillies and stir-fry for another 20 seconds. Then add the stock, rice wine or sherry, soy sauce, sugar and sesame oil. Cook over a high heat for 30 seconds, then return the meat to the wok and give the mixture several stirs to mix well. Turn onto a platter and serve at once, with plain rice and an easy soup.

Lionhead Pork Meatball Casserole
Shi Ti Tou

SERVES: 4

500 g (1 lb) fatty minced pork

1 egg white

4 tablespoons cold water

175 g (6 oz) fresh or canned water chestnuts, peeled if fresh, coarsely chopped

2 tablespoons light soy sauce

1 tablespoon dark soy sauce

2 tablespoons Shaoxing rice wine or dry sherry

1½ tablespoons sugar

2 teaspoons salt

½ teaspoon freshly ground black pepper

cornflour, for dusting

3–4 tablespoons groundnut or vegetable oil, plus 2 teaspoons

2 garlic cloves, crushed

500 g (1 lb) Chinese leaves, stalks separated, cut into 5 cm (2 inch) strips

450 ml (¾ pint) chicken stock

This popular dish from northern China with its distinctive texture is so named because the meatballs are said to resemble a lion's head and the cabbage leaves its mane.

1 Put the pork into a food processor and process with the egg white and cold water for 1 minute. The mixture should be light and fluffy. Do not use a blender, as it would make the mixture too dense. Then add the water chestnuts, soy sauces, rice wine or sherry, sugar, salt and pepper and process for another 30 seconds.

2 Divide the mixture into 8 equal amounts and roll each into a large meatball. Dust each meatball with cornflour. Heat a wok until it is hot, then add the 3–4 tablespoons oil. When the oil is hot and slightly smoking, add the meatballs, reduce the heat and slowly brown them. Remove the meatballs and set aside.

3 Clean the wok and reheat. When the wok is hot, add the remaining 2 teaspoons oil, then add the garlic and stir-fry for 10 seconds. Add the Chinese leaves and stir-fry for 20 seconds. Then add the stock and continue to cook for 2 minutes until the leaves are soft. Transfer the mixture to a heavy-based flameproof casserole. Lay the meatballs on top of the leaves and bring the mixture to the boil, then reduce the heat to very low, cover and simmer on a low heat for 1½ hours.

4 Arrange the leaves on a platter and lay the meatballs on top. Pour the sauce over the dish and serve at once.

Pearl Meatballs
Zhen Zhu Rou Wan

SERVES: 4

250 g (8 oz) white glutinous rice, soaked overnight

chopped fresh coriander, to garnish

MEATBALLS

500 g (1 lb) fatty minced pork

175 g (6 oz) fresh or canned water chestnuts, peeled if fresh, finely chopped

50 g (2 oz) cooked ham, finely diced

2 tablespoons light soy sauce

1 tablespoon Shaoxing rice wine or dry sherry

1 tablespoon peeled and finely chopped fresh root ginger

2 tablespoons finely chopped spring onions

1 teaspoon salt

2 teaspoons sugar

1 egg, beaten

1 tablespoon sesame oil

2 teaspoons roasted ground Sichuan peppercorns

2 teaspoons cornflour

Here, tasty meatballs are rolled in glutinous rice and steamed until they glisten like pearls, hence the name. Serve this dish as a starter or for parties.

1 Drain the rice and spread it out over a baking sheet.

2 Put all the ingredients for the meatballs in a bowl and mix well. Take about 2 tablespoons of the mixture and roll it between your palms into a ball about the size of a golf ball. Then roll this ball over the rice until the surface is covered. Repeat until you have used up all the mixture. Put the pearl meatballs on a heatproof plate.

3 Set up a steamer or put a rack into a wok or deep saucepan. Fill the steamer with about 5 cm (2 inches) of hot water. Bring the water to a simmer. Put the plate with the meatballs into the steamer or onto the rack. Cover the steamer, wok or pan tightly and gently steam over a medium heat for 15 minutes. Check the water and replenish it from time to time, as necessary. You will have to steam the pearl balls in 2 batches.

4 Arrange the pearl balls on a platter, garnish with chopped coriander and serve at once.

Pork Kidney in Aromatic Sauce
Guai Wei Yao Hua

SERVES: 4

500 g (1 lb) pigs' or lambs' kidneys

2 teaspoons bicarbonate of soda

1 tablespoon white vinegar or white rice vinegar

2 teaspoons salt

SAUCE

1½ tablespoons groundnut or vegetable oil

1 tablespoon finely chopped garlic

2 teaspoons peeled and finely chopped fresh root ginger

1 tablespoon dark soy sauce

1 tablespoon Shaoxing rice wine or dry sherry

1 tablespoon sugar

2 teaspoons light soy sauce

2 teaspoons black rice vinegar

2 teaspoons chilli bean sauce

1 teaspoon roasted ground Sichuan peppercorns

1 teaspoon sesame oil

1 teaspoon chilli oil

3 tablespoons finely chopped spring onions

The kidneys are stir-fried in a classic sauce, called 'strange-flavoured' in Chinese because it incorporates so many different tastes: hot, spicy, sour, sweet and salty.

1 Using a sharp knife, remove the thin outer membrane of the kidneys, then cut the kidneys horizontally in half. Cut away and discard the small knobs of fat and any tough membrane surrounding them. Score the kidneys by making light cuts in a criss-cross pattern over the surface without cutting right through them, then cut into 2.5 cm (1 inch) slices.

2 Combine the kidneys with the bicarbonate of soda and leave them to stand for 20 minutes (this helps to tenderize them and to neutralize their acidity). Rinse them thoroughly with cold water and toss them in the vinegar and salt to remove any remaining bitterness. Put them into a colander and leave them to drain for at least 30 minutes.

3 Blot the kidney slices dry with kitchen paper. Heat a wok over a high heat until it is hot, then add the groundnut or vegetable oil. When the oil is hot and slightly smoking, add the garlic and ginger and stir-fry for 20 seconds. Add the kidney and stir-fry for 1 minute. Add the rest of the ingredients and toss them well with the kidney. Continue to stir-fry the mixture for another 2 minutes or until the kidney edges begin to curl slightly.

4 Turn the mixture onto a serving platter and serve at once, with plain rice and stir-fried vegetables.

Shredded Pork in Bean Paste

Jing Du Rou Si

SERVES: 4

500 g (1 lb) lean pork, shredded

1½ tablespoons groundnut or vegetable oil

2 tablespoons finely chopped garlic

2 tablespoons ground yellow bean sauce

1 tablespoon Shaoxing rice wine or dry sherry

1 tablespoon hoisin sauce

4 whole spring onions, shredded

MARINADE

2 teaspoons dark soy sauce

2 teaspoons light soy sauce

2 teaspoons Shaoxing rice wine or dry sherry

½ teaspoon sugar

¼ teaspoon salt

1 teaspoon sesame oil

2 teaspoons cornflour

This quick and easy dish shows off the renowned Peking-inspired rich sauce, which is paired with the most popular Chinese meat – pork.

1 Put the pork and all the marinade ingredients in a bowl and mix well.

2 Heat a wok until it is hot, then add the oil. When the oil is hot and slightly smoking, add the pork and stir-fry for 1 minute. Add the garlic, bean sauce and rice wine or sherry and stir-fry for another minute. Then add the hoisin sauce and spring onions and continue to stir-fry for a further minute, mixing well.

3 Turn onto a platter and serve at once, with plain rice and your favourite vegetable dish.

Orange-flavoured Beef
Gui Zhou Niu Rou

SERVES: 4

500 g (1 lb) lean fillet or sirloin steak

3 tablespoons groundnut or vegetable oil

2 tablespoons finely chopped garlic

2 tablespoons peeled and finely chopped fresh root ginger

1 small onion, coarsely chopped

3 tablespoons Sichuan preserved vegetables, rinsed and finely chopped

2 large fresh red chillies, deseeded and finely shredded

2 tablespoons dried citrus peel, soaked in warm water for 20 minutes, drained and coarsely chopped, or finely grated fresh orange zest

2 tablespoons chicken stock

1½ tablespoons Shaoxing rice wine or dry sherry

1 tablespoon chilli bean sauce

1 tablespoon dark soy sauce

Beef, which plays a secondary role in Chinese cuisine, is enhanced with a distinctively flavoured marinade and then stir-fried with tart citrus peel in this Kweichow-inspired recipe.

1 Cut the beef into slices about 3 cm (1¼ inches) long and 5 mm (¼ inch) thick. Stack up the slices and finely shred the meat. Put the beef into a bowl, add all the marinade ingredients and mix well.

2 Heat a wok over a high heat until it is hot, then add the groundnut or vegetable oil. When the oil is very hot and begins to smoke, add the beef. Let the meat brown for 1 minute, then carefully stir-fry for another minute. Drain the beef in a colander, leaving 1 tablespoon oil in the wok.

2 teaspoons roasted
  ground Sichuan
  peppercorns
2 teaspoons sugar
2 teaspoons sesame oil
salt
chopped spring onions,
  to garnish

MARINADE
2 teaspoons light soy
  sauce
2 teaspoons dark soy
  sauce
1 tablespoon Shaoxing
  rice wine or dry
  sherry
2 teaspoons peeled and
  finely chopped fresh
  root ginger
2 teaspoons sesame oil
2 teaspoons salt
1 teaspoon sugar
2 teaspoons cornflour

3 Quickly reheat the wok and the oil. When it is hot, add the garlic and ginger and stir-fry for 20 seconds over a medium heat. Add the onion, preserved vegetables, fresh chillies and citrus peel or zest and stir-fry for another 20 seconds. Then add the stock, rice wine or sherry, chilli bean sauce, soy sauce, ground Sichuan peppercorns, sugar and sesame oil. Cook over a high heat for 30 seconds, then return the meat to the wok, add salt to taste and give the mixture several stirs to mix well.

4 Turn onto a platter, garnish with chopped spring onions and serve with rice, soup and a vegetable dish.

Minced Pork with Lettuce Leaves
Qi Cai Song

SERVES: 4–6

25 g (1 oz) Chinese dried mushrooms

1 large iceberg lettuce

500 g (1 lb) minced pork

1½ tablespoons groundnut or vegetable oil

2 tablespoons finely chopped garlic

125 g (4 oz) fresh or canned water chestnuts, peeled if fresh, chopped

1 red pepper, cored, deseeded and chopped

6 tablespoons finely chopped spring onions

1 tablespoon dark soy sauce

3 tablespoons oyster sauce

1 teaspoon sugar

MARINADE

1 tablespoon light soy sauce

1 tablespoon Shaoxing rice wine or dry sherry

½ teaspoon salt

1 teaspoon sugar

1 egg white

2 tablespoons cold chicken stock

2 teaspoon sesame oil

freshly ground black pepper, to taste

In this southern Chinese dish, a savoury pork mixture is enclosed in cool, crisp lettuce leaves and served with smoky mushrooms and a tasty oyster sauce.

1 Soak the mushrooms in warm water for 20 minutes, drain them and squeeze out any excess liquid. Remove and discard the stems and chop the caps. Carefully separate the lettuce leaves and arrange on a platter.

2 Put the pork and all the marinade ingredients in a bowl and mix well.

3 Heat a wok until it is hot, then add the oil. When the oil is hot and slightly smoking, add the pork mixture and stir-fry for 2 minutes. Add the garlic and stir-fry for a minute. Then add the water chestnuts, red pepper and spring onions and continue to stir-fry for 2 minutes until some of the liquid from the pork has evaporated. Add the soy sauce, oyster sauce and sugar and continue to stir-fry for 2 minutes over a high heat.

4 Mix well and serve with the lettuce leaves. Let each guest help him or herself by adding the mixture to the lettuce leaves. Serve as part of a Chinese meal with rice and other dishes.

Twice-cooked Pork
Hui Guo Rou

SERVES: 4

1 kg (2 lb) pork belly or
  meaty spareribs, cut
  into 5 cm (2 inch)
  pieces

4 slices of fresh root
  ginger, peeled

6 spring onions

2 tablespoons
  groundnut or
  vegetable oil

3 tablespoons finely
  chopped garlic

1 small onion, thinly
  sliced

1 red pepper, cored,
  deseeded and thinly
  sliced

1 green pepper, cored,
  deseeded and thinly
  sliced

250 g (8 oz) leeks, green
  part discarded,
  shredded

3 tablespoons chicken
  stock

2 tablespoons hoisin
  sauce

1 tablespoon chilli bean
  sauce

2 tablespoons Shaoxing
  rice wine or dry
  sherry

1 tablespoon dark soy
  sauce

1 teaspoon sugar

The flavour of pork is concentrated in the fat, but the problem with fatty meat is its chewy, greasy texture. Twice-cooking – simmering and stir-frying – is the age-old Chinese solution.

1 Bring a saucepan of salted water to the boil, add the belly or spareribs and simmer for 10 minutes, skimming the surface constantly to remove the scum. Add the ginger and spring onions. Reduce the heat to low, cover tightly and simmer for 30 minutes. Drain the meat thoroughly in a colander and discard the liquid and the aromatics.

2 Heat a wok over a high heat until it is hot, then add the oil. When the oil is hot and slightly smoking, add the meat and stir-fry for 5 minutes until the fat is rendered if using pork belly, or until brown.

3 Drain off any excess fat and oil, reserving 1 tablespoon. Add the garlic, onion, peppers and leeks and stir-fry for 4 minutes or until the vegetables are tender. Add the rest of the ingredients, then reduce the heat, cover and braise for 15 minutes until tender. Turn onto a platter and serve at once, with plain rice.

Beef and Mooli Stew

Luo Bo Po Niu Nan

SERVES: 4

1 kg (2 lb) beef brisket
(with some fat and
tendon), cut into 4 cm
(1½ inch) cubes

2 tablespoons
groundnut oil

2 tablespoons peeled
and finely chopped
fresh root ginger

4 spring onions, cut into
5 cm (2 inch) pieces

4 garlic cloves, whole
but lightly crushed

500 g (1 lb) mooli,
peeled and cut into
5 cm (2 inch) pieces

salt

chopped spring onions,
to garnish

BRAISING SAUCE

3 tablespoons Shaoxing
rice wine

2 tablespoons dark soy
sauce

1 tablespoon light soy
sauce

3 tablespoons hoisin
sauce

2 tablespoons ground
yellow bean sauce

2 tablespoons chilli
bean sauce

2 tablespoons
granulated sugar

3 whole star anise

½ teaspoon freshly
ground black pepper

1.2 litres (2 pints)
chicken stock

Inexpensive brisket is perfect here for the long cooking time, during which spices infuse the meat with complex flavours. Mooli (Chinese white radish) is often paired with beef. If you can't find mooli you can use turnips or carrots instead.

1 Bring a large saucepan of salted water to the boil. Add the meat and blanch for 10 minutes. Skim the surface constantly to remove all the scum and impurities. Drain the meat and discard the water.

2 Heat a wok until it is hot, then add the oil. When the oil is hot and slightly smoking, add the ginger, spring onions and garlic and stir-fry for 1 minute. Then add the beef and continue to stir-fry for 10 minutes or until the meat is brown. Drain off any excess fat or oil.

3 Transfer the meat to a large flameproof casserole or saucepan. Add all the braising sauce ingredients and bring to the boil. Reduce the heat, cover and simmer for 1½ hours or until the meat is tender. Add the mooli and continue to cook for another 30 minutes. Skim off any surface fat, garnish with chopped spring onions and serve immediately or cool and reheat to serve later. Plain rice is the perfect accompaniment.

Beef with Mangetout
Xue Dou Niu Rou Pian

SERVES: 4

500 g (1 lb) lean fillet or sirloin steak

2 teaspoons light soy sauce

1 tablespoon Shaoxing rice wine or dry sherry

4 teaspoons sesame oil

¼ teaspoon salt

pinch of sugar

2 teaspoons cornflour

3 tablespoons groundnut or vegetable oil

2 garlic cloves, lightly crushed

250 g (8 oz) fresh or canned baby corn

3 tablespoons chicken stock

250 g (8 oz) mangetout, trimmed

2 tablespoons oyster sauce

I have used lean beef here for this simple stir-fry because it is tender and low in fat. It again illustrates the Chinese penchant for contrasting colours, textures and flavours.

1 Cut the beef into slices about 3 cm (1¼ inches) long and 1 cm (½ inch) thick. Put the beef into a bowl and add the soy sauce, rice wine or sherry, 2 teaspoons sesame oil, salt, sugar and cornflour. Mix well and set aside.

2 Heat a wok over a high heat until it is hot, then add the groundnut or vegetable oil. When the oil is hot and slightly smoking, add the beef and stir-fry for 1½ minutes. Drain the beef in a colander, leaving 1 tablespoon oil in the wok.

3 Reheat the wok and the oil. When it is hot, add the garlic and stir-fry for 10 seconds over a medium heat. Add the corn and stock and cook over a high heat for 2 minutes. Then add the mangetout and continue to cook for another minute. Return the drained meat to the wok and stir to mix well. Add the oyster sauce and the remainder of the sesame oil and continue to stir-fry for 30 seconds. Give the mixture several stirs and then turn it on to a platter. Serve at once.

Savoury Deep-fried Wonton
Zha Huntun

MAKES: 30−35

250 g (8 oz) wonton skins

600 ml (1 pint) vegetable oil, for deep-frying

FILLING

375 g (12 oz) raw peeled prawns, deveined and chopped or coarsely minced

125 g (4 oz) minced fatty pork

2 teaspoons salt

½ teaspoon freshly ground white pepper

4 tablespoons finely chopped spring onions

2 teaspoons Shaoxing rice wine

1 teaspoon sugar

2 teaspoons sesame oil

1 egg white, lightly beaten

SWEET AND SOUR SAUCE

150 ml (¼ pint) water

2 tablespoons sugar

3 tablespoons white rice vinegar

3 tablespoons tomato purée or ketchup

1 teaspoon salt

½ teaspoon freshly ground white pepper

1 teaspoon cornflour, blended with 2 teaspoons water to a smooth paste

Prosaic wontons become savoury treats when dipped in a sweet and sour sauce. The sauce can be made a day in advance, refrigerated and brought to room temperature before serving.

1 For the filling, put the prawns and pork in a large bowl, add the salt and pepper and mix well, either by kneading with your hands or by stirring with a wooden spoon. Add all the other filling ingredients and stir well into the prawn and pork mixture. Cover the bowl with clingfilm and chill in the refrigerator for at least 20 minutes.

2 Meanwhile, combine all the sauce ingredients except the cornflour paste in a small saucepan. Bring the mixture to the boil, stir in the cornflour paste and cook for 1 minute. Leave to cool.

3 When you are ready to stuff the wontons, put 1 tablespoon of the filling in the centre of the first wonton skin. Dampen the edges with a little water and bring up the sides of the skin around the filling. Pinch the edges together at the top so that the wonton is sealed – it should look like a small filled bag.

4 Heat a wok over a high heat until it is hot, then add the oil for deep-frying. When the oil is hot and slightly smoking, add a handful of wontons and deep-fry for 3 minutes until golden and crispy. Remove with a slotted spoon and drain on kitchen paper. Continue to fry the remainder of the wontons. Serve them at once with the sweet and sour sauce.

Spring Rolls
Chun Juan

MAKES 15-20

- 1 packet spring roll skins, preferably the Shanghai type
- 25 g (1 oz) Chinese dried mushrooms
- 125 g (4 oz) raw peeled prawns, minced
- 125 g (4 oz) minced pork
- 1½ tablespoons groundnut or vegetable oil, plus 1.2 litres (2 pints) for deep-frying
- 2 tablespoons finely chopped garlic
- 1 tablespoon peeled and finely chopped fresh root ginger
- 1½ tablespoons light soy sauce
- 1 tablespoon Shaoxing rice wine or dry sherry
- 3 tablespoons finely chopped spring onions
- 1 teaspoon salt
- 1 teaspoon freshly ground black pepper
- 250 g (8 oz) Chinese leaves, finely shredded
- 1 egg, beaten
- Sweet and Sour Sauce (see page 62), to serve

There are two types of spring roll skins: the smooth, heavier, noodle-type Cantonese style and the transparent, lighter, rice paper-type Shanghai style, which I prefer.

1 If the spring roll skins are frozen, make sure that they are thawed thoroughly. Soak the mushrooms in warm water for 20 minutes, drain them and squeeze out any excess liquid. Remove and discard the stems and shred the caps.

2 Combine the prawns and pork with all the marinade ingredients in a small bowl.

3 Heat a wok over a high heat until it is hot, then add the 1½ tablespoons oil. When the oil is hot and slightly smoking, add the garlic and ginger and stir-fry for 20 seconds. Add the rest of the ingredients except the beaten egg and sauce and stir-fry for 5 minutes. Leave the mixture to cool thoroughly.

4 Place 3-4 tablespoons of the filling on each spring roll skin, fold in each side and roll up tightly. Use the beaten egg to seal the edge.

5 Clean the wok and reheat over a high heat until it is hot, then add the oil for deep-frying. When the oil is hot and slightly smoking, gently drop in as many spring rolls as will fit easily in one layer. Carefully fry the spring rolls for about 4 minutes until golden brown on the outside and cooked inside, adjusting the heat as necessary. Remove with a slotted spoon and drain on kitchen paper. You will need to cook the spring rolls in several batches.

1 teaspoon light soy
sauce

1 teaspoon Shaoxing
rice wine or dry
sherry

½ teaspoon salt

½ teaspoon cornflour

½ teaspoon sesame oil

¼ teaspoon freshly
ground black pepper

6 Serve them at once, hot and crispy, with the sweet and sour sauce on the side for dipping.

Poultry

Chicken with Walnuts
He Tao Ji Ding

SERVES: 4–6

500 g (1 lb) boneless, skinless chicken breasts, cut into 1 cm (½ inch) cubes

1 egg white

1 teaspoon salt

2 teaspoons cornflour

125 g (4 oz) shelled walnuts, halves or pieces

300 ml (½ pint) groundnut or vegetable oil

1 tablespoon finely chopped garlic

2 teaspoons peeled and finely chopped fresh root ginger

2 tablespoons finely chopped spring onions

1 tablespoon Shaoxing rice wine or dry sherry

1 tablespoon light soy sauce

2 teaspoons dark soy sauce

1 teaspoon sesame oil

chopped spring onions, to garnish

This classic stir-fry dish pairs the rich taste and crunchiness of walnuts with moist, delicately flavoured and silky textured chicken breast encased in egg white and cornflour.

1 Combine the chicken with the egg white, salt and cornflour in a small bowl, cover with clingfilm and chill in the refrigerator for about 20 minutes. Meanwhile, blanch the walnuts in boiling water for about 5 minutes, then drain thoroughly.

2 Heat a wok until it is hot, then add the groundnut or vegetable oil. When the oil is hot and slightly smoking, remove the wok from the heat. Add the chicken mixture, stir vigorously and leave in the warm oil for 3 minutes or until the chicken turns white. Drain immediately in a colander, reserving the oil.

3 Wipe the wok clean and reheat. When the wok is hot again, add 1 tablespoon of the drained oil (the remaining oil can be saved and reused for other chicken dishes). Quickly add the walnuts and stir-fry for 30 seconds. Add the garlic, ginger and spring onions and stir-fry for another 30 seconds.

4 Return the drained chicken to the wok and stir-fry for 1 minute. Then add the rice wine or sherry and soy sauces and continue to stir-fry for 2 minutes or until the chicken is cooked. Stir in the sesame oil. Garnish with spring onions and serve at once.

Boiled Chicken with Hot Sauce (Jiangxi)

Liu Lang Ji

SERVES: 4–6

one 1.5 kg–1.75 kg
(3–3½ lb) free-range
chicken

1 tablespoon salt

6 slices of fresh root
ginger

6 whole spring onions

1 tablespoon groundnut
or vegetable oil

2 teaspoons sesame oil

SAUCE

2 tablespoons finely
chopped garlic

2 large red chillies,
thinly sliced
(deseeded for a less
spicy sauce)

6 tablespoons finely
chopped spring
onions

2 tablespoons finely
chopped fresh
coriander

125 ml (4 fl oz) dark soy
sauce

1 tablespoon chilli bean
sauce

1 tablespoon Shaoxing
rice wine or dry
sherry

1 tablespoon white rice
vinegar

2 teaspoons sugar

freshly ground black
pepper

Here, the chicken is left to 'steep' in hot water, resulting in a delicate texture, succulence and full flavour, which marries nicely with a spicy northern-inspired sauce.

1 Rub the chicken evenly with the salt. Put the chicken in a saucepan large enough to hold it, cover with water and bring to the boil. Add the ginger and spring onions. Cover tightly, then reduce the heat and simmer for 20 minutes. Turn off the heat and leave, tightly covered, for 1 hour.

2 Place all the sauce ingredients in a stainless steel bowl and mix well. Heat a wok until it is hot, then add the oils. When the oils are very hot and smoking, pour them onto the sauce ingredients and mix well. Season to taste.

3 Remove the chicken to a chopping board. Strain and reserve the liquid (this can be used as a light stock). Carefully joint the chicken and arrange it on a platter. Pour the sauce over the chicken and serve at once.

Chicken in Lemon Sauce (Guangdong)
Ni Meng Ji

SERVES: 4–6

500 g (1 lb) boneless, skinless chicken breasts, cut into 1 cm (½ inch) cubes

1 egg white

1 teaspoon salt

2 teaspoons cornflour

125 ml (4 fl oz) groundnut or vegetable oil

1 tablespoon finely chopped garlic

6 tablespoons chicken stock

2 tablespoons fresh lemon juice

finely grated zest of 1 lemon

1 tablespoon Shaoxing rice wine or dry sherry

1 tablespoon sugar

1 tablespoon light soy sauce

2 tablespoons finely chopped spring onions

2 teaspoons cornflour, blended with 1 tablespoon water to a smooth paste

2 teaspoons sesame oil

chopped spring onions, to garnish

A favourite among diners in the West, this dish's origins are probably southern China, where it would most likely be made with dried tangerine peel, which has a much stronger taste.

1 Combine the chicken with the egg white, salt and cornflour in a small bowl, cover with clingfilm and chill in the refrigerator for about 20 minutes.

2 Heat a wok until it is hot, then add the groundnut or vegetable oil. When the oil is hot and slightly smoking, remove it from the heat. Add the chicken mixture, stir vigorously and leave to stand for 2 minutes or until the chicken turns white. Drain immediately in a colander, reserving the oil.

3 Wipe the wok clean and reheat. When the wok is hot again, return 1 tablespoon of the drained oil to it. When it is hot, add the garlic and stir-fry for 10 seconds or until it begins to brown. Add the rest of the ingredients except the cornflour paste and sesame oil. Bring the mixture to a simmer, then add the cornflour paste and simmer for another minute.

4 Return the chicken to the sauce and cook for 2 minutes, stirring to coat the pieces well with the sauce. Stir in the sesame oil. Turn onto a platter, garnish with chopped spring onions and serve at once.

Peking Duck and Flour Pancakes
Beijing Kao Ya and Bao Bing

SERVES 4-6

one 1.5 kg-1.75 kg
(3-3½ lb) Cherry
Valley duckling, fresh
or frozen

1.2 litres (2 pints) water

BASTING MIXTURE

4 tablespoons honey

3 tablespoons dark soy
sauce

3 tablespoons black rice
vinegar

PANCAKES

300 g (10 oz) plain flour,
plus extra for dusting

250-275 ml (8-9 fl oz)
very hot water

2 tablespoons sesame
oil

TO SERVE

6 spring onions,
shredded

6 tablespoons hoisin
sauce

Preparing Peking Duck in China is an art form, but I have devised a simpler method that closely approximates to the real thing – just give yourself plenty of time.

1 If the duck is frozen, leave it to thaw thoroughly. Rinse the duck well and blot it completely dry with kitchen paper. Insert a meat hook near the neck.

2 Bring the water to the boil in a large saucepan, then plunge the duck in several times. Let it drain well and hang it to dry in a cool place for 1 hour.

3 Add the basting mixture ingredients to the water and bring it to the boil. Reduce the heat to low and simmer for about 20 minutes. Using a large ladle or spoon, pour the mixture over the duck several times, as if to bathe it, until all the skin of the duck is completely coated with the mixture. Hang the duck in a cool, well-ventilated place to dry overnight, or alternatively hang it in front of a cold fan for at least 8 hours, longer if possible. Be sure to put a tray or roasting tin underneath to catch any drips. Once the duck has dried, the surface of the skin will feel like parchment.

4 Place the duck on a roasting rack in a roasting tin, breast-side up. Pour 150 ml (¼ pint) water into the tin, to prevent the fat from splattering. Roast the duck in a preheated oven, 240°C (475°F), Gas Mark 9, for 15 minutes. Reduce the heat to 180°C (350°F), Gas Mark 4, and continue to roast for 1 hour. Remove from the oven and leave to rest for at least 10 minutes before you carve it.

5 Meanwhile, for the pancakes, put the flour into a large bowl. Gradually stir in the hot water, mixing constantly with chopsticks or a fork until it is fully incorporated. Add more water if the mixture seems dry. Remove the dough from the bowl and knead it for 10 minutes with your hands, then put it back into the bowl, cover it with a clean, damp tea towel and leave to rest for about 30 minutes.

6 Remove the dough from the bowl and knead it again for about 5 minutes, dusting with a little flour if it is sticky. Once the dough is smooth, form it into a roll about 46 cm (18 inches) long and about 2.5 cm (1 inch) in diameter. Cut the roll into about 18 equal lengths with a knife. Roll each length into a ball.

7 Take 2 of the dough balls. Dip one side of one ball into the sesame oil and place the oiled side on top of the other ball. Take a rolling pin and roll both simultaneously into a round about 15 cm (6 inches) in diameter (this ensures that the dough remains moist inside and enables you to roll the pancakes thinner yet avoid overcooking them). Heat a wok or frying pan over a very low heat. Add the double pancake and cook until it has dried on one side. Flip it over and cook the other side. Remove from the pan, gently peel the 2 pancakes apart and set them aside. Repeat until all the dough balls have been cooked. Steam the pancakes to reheat them (don't use the oven, as this will dry them out too much), or alternatively, wrap them in clingfilm and reheat them for about 1 minute in a microwave oven. Wrap tightly in clingfilm to freeze, then let them thaw in the refrigerator first before reheating them.

8 Using a cleaver or a sharp knife, cut the duck skin and meat into pieces and arrange them on a warm platter. Serve at once with 8–12 pancakes, the spring onions and the hoisin sauce in a small bowl. Each guest spoons some sauce on to a pancake, puts a helping of crisp skin and meat on top with a spring onion 'brush', then rolls up the entire mixture in the pancake. It can be eaten using chopsticks or fingers.

Sichuan Cold Chicken Salad
Bang Bang Ji

SERVES: 4

375 g (12 oz) cucumber, peeled, deseeded and thinly sliced widthways

1½ teaspoons salt

600 ml (1 pint) chicken stock or water

2 whole spring onions

4 slices of fresh root ginger

500 g (1 lb) boneless, skinless chicken breasts

chopped spring onions, to garnish

SAUCE

1½ tablespoons sesame paste or creamy peanut butter

1½ tablespoons light soy sauce

2 teaspoons dark soy sauce

1 tablespoon sugar

1 tablespoon chilli oil

1 tablespoon white rice vinegar

1½ tablespoons sugar

2 teaspoons roasted ground Sichuan peppercorns

2 teaspoons sesame oil

The name is derived from the beating of the chicken meat, birds traditionally being rather scrawny and leathery, to make it tender. This makes a terrific summer lunch dish.

1 Put the cucumber in a colander and mix with the salt. Leave to stand for 15 minutes. Put the cucumber in a linen cloth and squeeze as much liquid as you can from the cucumber. Arrange on a platter and set aside.

2 Bring the stock or water to a simmer in a small saucepan, add the whole spring onions, ginger and chicken and simmer for 5 minutes. Remove the pan from the heat, cover tightly and leave to stand undisturbed for 15 minutes. Remove the chicken with a slotted spoon and leave to cool. Reserve the stock for future use.

3 Mix all the sauce ingredients together in a bowl and set aside.

4 Tear the meat into long strips with your hands. Arrange the chicken on top of the cucumber, evenly distribute the sauce and garnish with chopped spring onions. Serve at once.

Stewed Chicken in Oyster Sauce
Shen Xian Hao You Ji

SERVES: 2−4

25 g (1 oz) Chinese dried mushrooms

500 g (1 lb) boneless, skinless chicken thighs, cut into 4 cm (1½ inch) pieces

2 tablespoons groundnut or vegetable oil

1½ tablespoons finely chopped garlic

2 teaspoons peeled and finely chopped fresh root ginger

3 tablespoons oyster sauce

2 tablespoons Shaoxing rice wine or dry sherry

2 teaspoons light soy sauce

2 teaspoons dark soy sauce

1 teaspoon sesame oil

250 ml (8 fl oz) chicken stock

chopped spring onions, to garnish

MARINADE

1 teaspoon salt

½ teaspoon freshly ground black pepper

1 tablespoon light soy sauce

2 teaspoons Shaoxing rice wine

1 teaspoon sesame oil

2 teaspoons cornflour

In this seemingly unlikely combination, the savoury oyster sauce (which, remember, does not taste fishy) adds a subtle, rich flavour that enhances the delicate qualities of the chicken.

1 Soak the mushrooms in warm water for 20 minutes, drain them and squeeze out any excess liquid. Remove the stems and discard and quarter the caps.

2 Combine the chicken with the marinade ingredients in a bowl, cover with clingfilm and leave to marinate for 20 minutes.

3 Heat a wok over a high heat until it is hot, then add the groundnut or vegetable oil. When the oil is hot and slightly smoking, add the chicken and stir-fry for 5 minutes or until the chicken is brown. Drain in a colander, reserving the oil, and then transfer the chicken to a flameproof casserole.

4 Do not wipe out the wok. Reheat over a medium heat and add 1 tablespoon of the drained oil. When it is hot, add the garlic and ginger and stir-fry for 10 seconds. Add the oyster sauce, rice wine or sherry, soy sauces, sesame oil and stock. Bring the mixture to the boil and add the mushrooms. Transfer to the casserole with the chicken.

5 Bring the mixture to a simmer, cover tightly and cook over a low heat for 15 minutes. Transfer to a platter, garnish with chopped spring onions and serve.

Crispy Shredded Duck
Xiang Su Ya

SERVES: 4

one 1.5 kg–1.75 kg (3–3½ lb) Cherry Valley duckling, fresh or frozen

3 tablespoons dark soy sauce

cornflour, for dusting

1.2 litres (2 pints) groundnut or vegetable oil, for deep-frying

MARINADE

2 tablespoons sea salt

1 tablespoon five-spice powder

1 tablespoon roasted ground Sichuan peppercorns

4 tablespoons Shaoxing rice wine or dry sherry

6 whole spring onions

12 slices of fresh root ginger

TO SERVE

Flour Pancakes (see pages 74–77)

shredded spring onions

hoisin sauce

This ever-popular dish takes time to make properly, but it is worth the effort. Steaming eliminates most of the duck's fat, while the deep-frying gives it its characteristic crisp texture.

1 If the duck is frozen, leave it to thaw thoroughly. Rinse it well and blot it completely dry with kitchen paper.

2 Mix the salt, five-spice powder, Sichuan peppercorns and rice wine or sherry in a bowl. Rub this over the inside and outside of the duck. Put the spring onions and ginger inside the duck cavity. Cover with clingfilm and leave to marinate in the refrigerator for 8 hours or overnight.

3 Put the duck in a deep, heatproof dish. Set up a steamer or put a rack into a wok or deep saucepan. Fill the steamer, work or pan with about 5 cm (2 inches) of hot water. Bring the water to a simmer. Put the dish with the duck into the steamer or onto the rack. Cover the steamer, wok or pan tightly and gently steam over a medium heat for 2 hours. Replenish the water from time to time and empty the considerable amount of fat that will collect and discard.

4 Gently remove the duck from the steamer, wok or pan and leave to stand for at least 1 hour until cool. Using a cleaver or a sharp knife, cut the duck in half. Rub the skin with the soy sauce and dust with cornflour.

5 Heat a wok over a high heat until it is hot, then add the oil for deep-frying. When the oil is hot and slightly smoking, deep-fry half the duck on the skin side for 3 minutes until the skin is crispy and brown. Drain on kitchen paper. Deep-fry the other half. Leave the duck to cool for 5 minutes, then remove and shred the skin and meat, arrange it on a platter and serve with Flour Pancakes, shredded spring onions and hoisin sauce.

Chicken in Black Bean Sauce

Luo Ding Dou Chi Ji

SERVES: 2−4

500 g (1 lb) boneless, skinless chicken thighs, cut into 2.5 cm (1 inch) pieces

1 tablespoon groundnut or vegetable oil

3 tablespoons finely chopped shallots

2 tablespoons black beans, coarsely chopped

1½ tablespoons finely chopped garlic

1 tablespoon peeled and finely chopped fresh root ginger

1 tablespoon Shaoxing rice wine or dry sherry

2 teaspoons light soy sauce

2 teaspoons dark soy sauce

150 ml (¼ pint) chicken stock

2 teaspoons sesame oil

3 tablespoons finely chopped spring onions

MARINADE

1 tablespoon light soy sauce

1 tablespoon Shaoxing rice wine or dry sherry

½ teaspoon salt

½ teaspoon sugar

1 teaspoon sesame oil

2 teaspoons cornflour

This classic southern Chinese dish has travelled the world, finding a warm reception everywhere. The pungent aromatic black beans are an ideal complement to the delicate chicken flavour.

1 Put the chicken with all marinade ingredients into a glass bowl and mix well. Cover with clingfilm and set aside for 15 minutes.

2 Heat a wok over a high heat until it is hot, then add the groundnut or vegetable oil. When the oil is hot and slightly smoking, add the chicken and stir-fry for 5 minutes until lightly browned. Add the shallots, black beans, garlic and ginger and stir-fry for another minute. Add the rice wine or sherry, soy sauces and stock and continue to cook over a high heat for 2 minutes, then stir in the sesame oil and spring onions.

3 Turn onto a platter and serve at once, with plain rice and a simple stir-fried vegetable dish.

General Tang's Chicken
Zuo Zong Tang Ji

The influences of Hunan, a province in southern China well known for its fiery cuisine, are obvious in the spicy yet sweet flavours of this dish – it certainly has 'tang'!

SERVES: 4

500 g (1 lb) boneless, skinless chicken thighs, cut into 2.5 cm (1 inch) pieces

1.2 litres (2 pints) groundnut or vegetable oil, for deep-frying

MARINADE

1 teaspoon salt

½ teaspoon freshly ground black pepper

1 tablespoon light soy sauce

2 teaspoons Shaoxing rice wine or dry sherry

1 teaspoon sesame oil

2 teaspoons cornflour

BATTER

2 tablespoons cornflour

50 g (2 oz) plain flour

1 teaspoon baking powder

150 ml (¼ pint) water

½ teaspoon salt

1 teaspoon groundnut or vegetable oil

1 teaspoon sesame oil

1 Combine the chicken with all the marinade ingredients in a glass bowl, cover with clingfilm and leave to marinate for 20 minutes.

2 Blend all the batter ingredients together in a blender until it is smooth with *no* lumps. Strain the batter through a sieve if necessary. Combine the batter with the chicken.

3 For the sauce, heat a saucepan over a medium heat until it is hot and add the oil. When the oil is hot and slightly smoking, add the chillies and garlic and stir-fry for 30 seconds or until the garlic begins to brown. Add the salt, sugar, stock or water and vinegar and bring the mixture to the boil. Add the cornflour paste and return to the boil. Reduce the heat to low and simmer, uncovered, for 10 minutes.

4 Heat a wok over a high heat until it is hot, then add the oil for deep-frying. When the oil is hot and slightly smoking, remove the chicken from the batter with tongs and deep-fry in 2 or 3 batches until golden and crispy. Drain well on kitchen paper and set on a warm platter. Immediately pour the sauce over the chicken and serve at once, with plain rice and a vegetable dish.

SAUCE

1½ tablespoons
   groundnut or
   vegetable oil

5 dried red chillies,
   halved

5 garlic cloves, finely
   sliced

1 teaspoon salt

3 tablespoons sugar

300 ml (½ pint) chicken
   stock or water

2 teaspoons white rice
   vinegar

1 teaspoon cornflour,
   blended with
   1 teaspoon water
   to a smooth paste

Portuguese Chicken (Hong Kong)
Pu Guo Ji

SERVES: 4

500 g (1 lb) boneless,
skinless chicken thighs

250 g (8 oz) carrots

250 g (8 oz) potatoes

1½ tablespoons
groundnut oil

1 tablespoon peeled and
finely chopped fresh
root ginger

2 teaspoons finely
chopped garlic

1 tablespoon light soy
sauce

1 tablespoon dark soy
sauce

1 tablespoon Shaoxing
rice wine

3 tablespoons Madras
curry paste

1 tablespoon sugar

1 teaspoon salt

400 ml (14 fl oz) canned
coconut milk

200 ml (7 fl oz) chicken
stock

freshly ground black
pepper

chopped spring onions,
to garnish

MARINADE

1½ tablespoons light soy
sauce

2 teaspoons dark soy
sauce

1½ tablespoons rice wine

2 teaspoons salt

2 teaspoons sesame oil

2 teaspoons cornflour

This dish, popular in both Macao and Hong Kong, is clearly an amalgam of South-east Asian styles and Portuguese predilections. The coconut milk adds a rich, sweet flavour.

1 Cut the chicken into 2.5 cm (1 inch) pieces and mix well with all the marinade ingredients in a glass bowl. Cover with clingfilm and leave to marinate in the refrigerator for 1 hour. Drain well and reserve the marinade.

2 Peel the carrots and potatoes and cut into 5 cm (2 inch) pieces, then set aside.

3 Heat a wok over a high heat until it is hot, then add the oil. When the oil is hot and slightly smoking, add the ginger and garlic and stir-fry for 20 seconds. Add the chicken and stir-fry for 3 minutes or until the chicken is lightly browned.

4 Transfer the contents of the wok to a large saucepan, then add the rest of the ingredients, including the reserved marinade and vegetables, and bring to the boil. Reduce the heat and simmer for 20 minutes. Garnish with chopped spring onions and serve at once, with plain rice.

Sichuan Chicken

Gong Bao Ji Ding

SERVES: 4

500 g (1 lb) boneless, skinless chicken breasts, cut into 1 cm (½ inch) cubes

1 egg white

1 teaspoon salt

2 teaspoons cornflour

300 ml (½ pint) groundnut or vegetable oil

2 dried chillies, halved

125 g (4 oz) shelled, skinned raw or roasted peanuts

1 tablespoon finely chopped garlic

1 teaspoon peeled and finely chopped fresh root ginger

2 tablespoons finely chopped spring onions

2 tablespoons Shaoxing rice wine or dry sherry

2 tablespoons dark soy sauce

2 teaspoons chilli bean sauce

2 teaspoons black rice vinegar

2 teaspoons sugar

1 teaspoon cornflour, blended with 1 tablespoon water to a smooth paste

1 teaspoon sesame oil

This Sichuan classic has become well known to Chinese food lovers throughout the world. It is easy to see why – hot, sour, sweet and salty flavours meld together delightfully.

1 Combine the chicken with the egg white, salt and cornflour in a small bowl, cover with clingfilm and chill in the refrigerator for about 20 minutes.

2 Heat a wok until it is hot, then add the groundnut or vegetable oil. When the oil is hot and slightly smoking, remove the wok from the heat. Add the chicken mixture, stir vigorously and leave in the warm oil for 3 minutes or until the chicken turns white. Drain immediately in a colander, reserving the oil.

3 Wipe the wok clean and reheat. When the wok is hot again, add 1½ tablespoons of the drained oil (the remaining oil can be saved and reused for other chicken dishes). Quickly add the dried chillies and peanuts and stir-fry for 30 seconds. Allow the chillies to blacken and the peanuts to lightly brown, to flavour the oil. Add the garlic, ginger and spring onions and stir-fry for another 30 seconds.

4 Return the drained chicken to the wok and stir-fry for 1 minute. Add the rice wine or sherry, soy sauce, chilli bean sauce, vinegar and sugar and continue to stir-fry for 2 minutes or until the chicken is cooked. Add the cornflour paste and cook until the sauce has thickened. Add the sesame oil, give the mixture a good stir and serve at once.

Paper-wrapped Chicken
Zhi Bao Ji Pian

SERVES: 4–6

250 g (8 oz) boneless, skinless chicken breasts

30 shreds of red chillies

60 fresh coriander leaves

30 pieces of cooked ham, cut into 8 cm (3¼ inch) squares

60 shreds of spring onion

30 shreds of peeled fresh root ginger

30 pieces of thinly sliced fresh, peeled or canned water chestnuts

1.2 litres (2 pints) groundnut or vegetable oil, for deep-frying

MARINADE

2 tablespoons oyster sauce

1 tablespoon light soy sauce

1 tablespoon dark soy sauce

1 tablespoon Shaoxing rice wine or dry sherry

2 teaspoons sugar

1 teaspoon sesame oil

salt and freshly ground black pepper

This method of cooking chicken is ingenious: a thin slice of chicken is sandwiched between flavourful ingredients, wrapped in greaseproof paper and deep-fried to make a delicious, unique starter.

1 Cut the chicken into 30 thin pieces and combine it with all the marinade ingredients in a glass bowl. Cover with clingfilm and leave to marinate in the refrigerator for at least 1 hour.

2 Place a 15 cm (6 inch) square of greaseproof paper on a work surface with a corner towards you, then fold the tip of the corner in slightly. Put in the centre of the paper square the following: a shred of chilli, a coriander leaf, a piece each of chicken and ham, 2 shreds of spring onion, a shred of ginger, a slice of water chestnut and finally another coriander leaf. Fold the first corner over the ingredients, then fold in the sides. Fold the entire package in half, leaving a flap at the corner furthest from you. Finally, fold the flap over the folded-up package to secure. Repeat until all the packages are filled.

3 Heat a wok over a high heat until it is hot, then add the oil for deep-frying. When the oil is hot and slightly smoking, add about 10 packages and deep-fry for about 3 minutes. Remove with a slotted spoon and drain well on kitchen paper. Deep-fry the remaining packages in 2 batches in the same manner.

4 Arrange the packages on a platter and let each of your guests unwrap his or her own packages.

Five-spiced Tea Eggs
Wu Syang Cha Ye Dan

SERVES: 4−6

1.8 litres (3 pints) water

6 eggs, at room
temperature

TEA-LIQUID
MIXTURE

500 ml (17 fl oz) water

2 tablespoons Chinese
black tea

2 tablespoons dark soy
sauce

1 tablespoon light soy
sauce

2 teaspoons five-spice
powder

1 teaspoon roasted
ground Sichuan
peppercorns

1 teaspoon salt

*Eggs are rarely eaten as a plain dish by themselves in Chinese
cuisine, but they do lend themselves to imaginative combinations.
These marbled eggs are one such unusual and delicious treat.*

1 Bring the water to the boil in large saucepan, add the
eggs and cook for 10 minutes. Remove the eggs and
immediately plunge them in cold water, then gently crack
the shells with a large spoon under cold running water
until the entire shell is a network of cracks. Leave them
in the cold running water for at least 10 minutes.

2 Bring all the ingredients for the tea-liquid mixture
to a simmer in a saucepan, then add the cracked eggs to
the pan. Cook for 10 minutes, then remove the pan from
the heat and leave the eggs in the liquid to cool. If you
have the time, leave the eggs in the liquid overnight in
the refrigerator.

3 When you are ready to serve the eggs, gently peel off
the cracked shells and serve.

Fish

Stir-fried Prawns with Peas
Ching Dou Hsia Ren

SERVES: 4

500 g (1 lb) large, shell-on raw prawns

2 teaspoons salt

300 ml (½ pint) cold water

1 small egg white

1 teaspoon cornflour

150 ml (¼ pint) groundnut or vegetable oil

1 tablespoon finely chopped garlic

125 g (4 oz) frozen peas

3 tablespoons chicken stock

1 tablespoon Shaoxing rice wine or dry sherry

2 teaspoons light soy sauce

1 teaspoon sugar

1 teaspoon cornflour, blended with 1 teaspoon water to a smooth paste

1 teaspoon sesame oil

This Shanghai-inspired dish is simple to make. Washing the prawns first in salt water cleans and firms their flesh, and the peas provide a sweet foil to their richness.

1 Peel the prawns. Using a small, sharp knife, make a shallow cut down the back of each prawn and remove the black thread. Mix the salt with the cold water and use to wash the prawns. Rinse well and pat dry with kitchen paper.

2 Combine the prawns with the egg white and cornflour in a bowl. Cover with clingfilm and chill in the refrigerator for at least 15 minutes.

3 Heat a wok until it is hot, then add the groundnut or vegetable oil. When the oil is hot and slightly smoking, remove from the heat. Add the prawns, quickly stir to separate them and then leave in the oil for 2 minutes. Drain in a colander and discard all but 1 tablespoon of the oil.

4 Reheat the wok and the oil. When it is hot, add the garlic and stir-fry for 10 seconds. Then add the peas and stir-fry for 1 minute. Add the stock, rice wine or sherry, soy sauce and sugar. Stir to mix well and cook for 30 seconds.

5 Stir in the cornflour paste and cook for 10 seconds. Return the prawns to the mixture and stir to coat well. When the prawns are heated through, stir in the sesame oil and serve at once, with rice and a stir-fried vegetable dish.

Fish Fillets Fried with Ginger
Chao Yu Pian

SERVES: 2–4

500 g (1 lb) sole or plaice fillets, skinned and left whole

1 teaspoon salt

½ teaspoon freshly ground white pepper

cornflour, for dusting

1 egg, beaten

125 ml (4 fl oz) groundnut or vegetable oil, plus 1 tablespoon

3 tablespoons peeled and finely shredded fresh root ginger

2 tablespoons Shaoxing rice wine or dry sherry

2 teaspoons light soy sauce

1½ teaspoons sugar

3 tablespoons chicken stock or water

2 teaspoons sesame oil

chopped spring onions, for garnish

Using aromatic ginger with fish is a Chinese favourite. I like using a delicate fish like sole here, but take not to overcook it or break it up.

1 Sprinkle the fish fillets evenly on both sides with half the salt and pepper. Dust them with cornflour, shaking off any excess. Dip each fillet in the beaten egg and again dust with cornflour.

2 Heat a wok over a high heat until it is hot, then add the 125 ml (4 fl oz) groundnut or vegetable oil. When the oil is hot and slightly smoking, reduce the heat to medium and slowly fry the fillets on each side until they are golden. This should take 2–3 minutes. Drain them on a baking sheet lined with kitchen paper. Drain off all the oil and discard. Clean the wok and wipe it dry.

3 Reheat the wok over a high heat until it is hot, then add the 1 tablespoon oil. When the oil is hot and slightly smoking, add the ginger. Stir-fry for 20 seconds, then add the rice wine or sherry, soy sauce, sugar, stock or water and the remaining salt and white pepper. Cook over a high heat for 30 seconds.

4 Return the fish fillets to the wok and gently coat them with the sauce for 1 minute, taking care not to break them up. Drizzle the sesame oil on top, then remove to a platter, garnish with chopped spring onions and serve at once, with vegetables and rice.

Spicy Braised Fish
Gan Shao Yu

SERVES: 4–6

1 whole fish, 1.25–1.5 kg
(2½–3 lb), or 2
haddock or halibut
fish fillets, about 500 g
(1 lb) each

2 teaspoons salt

cornflour, for dusting

2 eggs, beaten

600 ml (1 pint)
groundnut or
vegetable oil

chopped fresh
coriander, to garnish

SAUCE

1½ tablespoons
groundnut or
vegetable oil

2 tablespoons finely
chopped garlic

2 tablespoons peeled
and finely chopped
fresh root ginger

2 tablespoons finely
chopped shallots

2 tablespoons Shaoxing
rice wine or dry
sherry

2 tablespoons whole
yellow bean sauce

1½ tablespoons dark
soy sauce

1 tablespoon light soy
sauce

A whole fish is a symbol of prosperity and good luck, and thus reserved for special occasions. This dish is a favourite, as delicious as it is elegant.

1 Put the fish on a baking sheet. Make 3 slanted cuts on each side of the fish, to help it cook evenly. Sprinkle the salt and cornflour evenly over each side of the fish. Shake off any excess cornflour. Baste the fish with the beaten egg and again coat each side with cornflour, shaking off any excess.

2 Heat a wok over a high heat until it is hot, then add the 600 ml (1 pint) groundnut or vegetable oil. When the oil is slightly smoking, slide the fish in and deep-fry for 4 minutes or until golden brown. Then carefully turn the fish over and fry the other side. Remove the fish and drain on kitchen paper. Discard the oil and wipe out the wok.

3 Reheat the wok over a high heat until it is hot, then add the 1½ tablespoons groundnut or vegetable oil. When the oil is hot and slightly smoking, add the garlic, ginger and shallots and stir-fry for 20 seconds. Add the rest of the sauce ingredients except the stock, cornflour paste, spring onions and sesame oil. Stir-fry this mixture for 1 minute, then add the stock and cornflour paste, and when it boils, reduce the heat. Carefully slide the fish into the sauce and baste constantly while cooking. Continue to cook for 5 minutes or until the fish is cooked through.

4 Carefully remove the fish and arrange on a platter. Add the spring onions and sesame oil to the sauce, then pour over the fish and garnish with chopped coriander. Serve at once, with plain rice and a vegetable dish.

1 tablespoon chilli bean
 sauce

2 teaspoons sugar

450 ml (¾ pint) chicken
 stock

2 teaspoons cornflour,
 blended with
 1 tablespoon water
 to a smooth paste

3 tablespoons finely
 chopped spring
 onions

2 teaspoons sesame oil

Fish Steamed with Black Beans
Dou Shr Jeng Hsien Yu

SERVES: 4

625 g (1¼ lb) haddock fillet, skinned and divided into 4 equal pieces

1 teaspoon salt

¼ teaspoon freshly ground white pepper

2 tablespoons black beans, chopped

1½ tablespoons finely chopped garlic

1 tablespoon peeled and finely chopped fresh root ginger

1 tablespoon Shaoxing rice wine or dry sherry

1 tablespoon light soy sauce

3 tablespoons finely chopped spring onions

3 tablespoons roughly chopped fresh coriander

1 tablespoon groundnut or vegetable oil

2 teaspoons sesame oil

Here is a classic method of steaming fish – with black beans, which add zest and pungent seasoning without overwhelming the delicate character of the fish.

1 Rub the fish fillets evenly with the salt and pepper. Combine the black beans, garlic and ginger in a small bowl. Put the fish fillets on a heatproof plate, evenly scatter the black bean mixture over the top, then pour over the rice wine or sherry and soy sauce.

2 Set up a steamer or put a rack into a wok or deep saucepan. Fill the steamer, wok or pan with about 5 cm (2 inches) of hot water. Bring the water to a simmer. Put the plate with the fish into the steamer or onto the rack. Cover the steamer, wok or pan tightly and gently steam over a medium heat for 8–10 minutes, depending on the thickness of the fillets. Replenish the water from time to time. When the fish is cooked, remove the plate from the steamer, wok or pan. Scatter the spring onions and coriander on top of the fish.

3 Heat a wok until it is hot, then add the oils. When the oils are very hot and start to smoke, pour over the fish fillets. Serve at once with plain rice and a stir-fried vegetable dish for a complete meal.

Batter-fried Butterfly Prawns
Feng Wei Xia

SERVES: 4–6

500 g (1 lb) raw king prawns, peeled and deveined but tails left intact

cornflour, for dusting

2 large eggs, beaten

1 teaspoon salt

½ teaspoon freshly ground white pepper

1 teaspoon sesame oil

dried breadcrumbs, for coating

300 ml (½ pint) groundnut or vegetable oil

2 lemons, sliced into wedges, to garnish

roasted Sichuan peppercorns, ground and combined with salt, to serve

The popularity that this dish enjoys in the West is growing in China, with good reason – deep-frying preserves the prawn's moistness and the batter provides crunchiness.

1 To butterfly the prawns, make a deep cut down the belly of each prawn and then open it out. Wash the prawns and pat them dry with kitchen paper. Lay them out on a baking sheet and dust them evenly with the cornflour.

2 Combine the beaten eggs, salt, pepper and sesame oil in a glass bowl. Dip each prawn in the egg mixture and then roll them in the breadcrumbs.

3 Heat a wok until it is hot, then add the groundnut or vegetable oil. When the oil is hot and slightly smoking, fry the prawns for about 2 minutes until they are golden brown. Drain them on kitchen paper and serve at once, garnished with the lemon wedges, with a small bowl of roasted Sichuan pepper and salt on the side.

Sweet and Sour Fish
Tang Cu Quan Yu

SERVES: 4

2 haddock or halibut fillets, about 250 g (8 oz) each

2 teaspoons salt

cornflour, for dusting

1 egg, beaten

600 ml (1 pint) groundnut or vegetable oil, plus 1 tablespoon

2 tablespoons finely chopped garlic

2 tablespoons peeled and finely chopped fresh root ginger

1 small onion, sliced

125 g (4 oz) frozen peas

SAUCE

2 tablespoons Shaoxing rice wine

1 tablespoon dark soy sauce

1 tablespoon light soy sauce

2 tablespoons tomato purée or ketchup

2 teaspoons salt

2 tablespoons sugar

150 ml (¼ pint) chicken stock

5 tablespoons white rice vinegar

2 teaspoons cornflour, blended with 1 tablespoon water to a smooth paste

This recipe is popular in eastern and southern China, where seafood is abundant. The sweet and pungent flavours of the sauce combine well with the firm and succulent fish.

1 Put the fish fillets on a baking sheet. Sprinkle the salt and cornflour evenly over each side of the fish. Shake off any excess cornflour. Baste the fish with the beaten egg and again coat each side with cornflour, shaking off any excess.

2 Heat a wok over a high heat until it is hot, then add the 600 ml (1 pint) oil. When the oil is slightly smoking, slide the fish fillets in and deep-fry for 4 minutes or until golden brown. Carefully turn them over and fry the other side. Remove the fish and drain on kitchen paper. Discard the oil and wipe out the wok.

3 Reheat the wok over a high heat until it is hot, then add the 1 tablespoon oil. When the oil is hot and slightly smoking, add the garlic, ginger and onion and stir-fry for 20 seconds. Then add the peas and continue to stir-fry for 2 minutes.

4 Add all the sauce ingredients except the cornflour paste. Bring the mixture to the boil, then add the cornflour paste and cook until thickened. Reduce the heat to a simmer, carefully slide the fish fillets into the sauce and baste constantly while cooking. Continue to cook for 5 minutes or until the fish is cooked through.

5 Carefully remove the fish and arrange on a platter. Pour the sauce over the fish and serve at once. This dish goes well with other Chinese meat or vegetable dishes you may wish to serve at the same time.

Prawn Toast
Zha Xia Bao

SERVES: 4 AS
AN APPETIZER
OR 8 AS A
COCKTAIL
SNACK

8 thin slices of white bread, crusts removed, cut into quarters

250 g (8 oz) raw peeled prawns, minced

50 g (1 oz) minced fatty pork

1 teaspoon peeled and finely chopped fresh root ginger

2 tablespoons finely chopped spring onions, white part only

1 teaspoon Shaoxing rice wine or dry sherry

½ teaspoon sesame oil

1 egg white, lightly beaten

½ teaspoon cornflour

1 teaspoon salt

½ teaspoon freshly ground white pepper

400 ml (14 fl oz) groundnut or vegetable oil

This savoury snack is often served as part of dim sum in Chinese restaurants outside of China. Drying out the bread prevents it from soaking up the oil.

1 Place the bread on a baking sheet and put in a preheated oven, 120°C (250°F), Gas Mark ½, for 5 minutes, then turn the bread over and return to the oven for another 5 minutes. Remove the bread and leave it to cool.

2 Put the prawns, pork, ginger, spring onions and rice wine or sherry into a food processor or blender and mix for 30 seconds. Then add the sesame oil, egg white, cornflour, salt and pepper and blend until smooth.

3 Spread the paste onto the pieces of dried bread, to about 5 mm (¼ inch) thick, and set aside.

4 Heat a wok until it is hot, then add the groundnut or vegetable oil. When the oil is hot and slightly smoking, put about 4 pieces of the prawn toast, paste-side down, in the oil and deep-fry for about 3 minutes. Turn over and continue to deep-fry for another minute or until they are golden brown. Remove with a slotted spoon and drain on kitchen paper. Repeat the process until all the prawn toasts are cooked. Serve at once.

Prawn Crackers
Xia Pian

SERVES: 4

125 g (4 oz) **dried prawn crackers**

600 ml (1 pint) **groundnut or vegetable oil**

Try these prawn crackers as a wonderful alternative to the usual crisps, nachos or crackers as an ideal snack to serve with drinks, or use to garnish any dish. Dried prawn crackers come in many different shapes and colours, but I prefer the natural pink ones.

1 Heat a wok over a high heat until it is hot, then add the oil. When the oil is hot and slightly smoking, test the oil by dropping a dried prawn cracker in the oil. It should puff up and float to the surface immediately.

2 When the oil is ready, drop a handful of the crackers in, scoop them out immediately with a slotted spoon and drain them on a baking sheet lined with kitchen paper. Repeat until they have all been fried.

3 The oil can be saved and used for cooking fish or prawn dishes (do not use for any other dishes); simply leave it to cool and then filter it through a muslin or fine sieve into a jar. Cover tightly and keep in a cool, dry place. If kept in the refrigerator it will become cloudy, but it will clarify again when the oil returns to room temperature.

Red-cooked Fish
Hong Shao Yu

SERVES: 4

2 haddock or halibut
   fillets, about 250 g
   (8 oz) each

2 teaspoons salt

cornflour, for dusting

3 tablespoons
   groundnut or
   vegetable oil

chopped spring onions,
   to garnish

SAUCE

1½ tablespoons
   groundnut or
   vegetable oil

1 tablespoon finely
   chopped garlic

1 tablespoon peeled and
   finely chopped fresh
   root ginger

2 tablespoons Shaoxing
   rice wine or dry
   sherry

1½ tablespoons hoisin
   sauce

1 tablespoon dark soy
   sauce

2 teaspoons ground
   yellow bean sauce

1 tablespoon rock sugar
   or ordinary sugar

150 ml (¼ pint) chicken
   stock

2 teaspoons cornflour,
   blended with
   1 tablespoon water
   to a smooth paste

2 teaspoons sesame oil

The fish is first pan-fried and then braised only briefly in the sauce to ensure that its texture is preserved while its taste is enhanced and flesh beautifully coloured.

1 Put the fish fillets on a baking sheet. Sprinkle the salt and cornflour evenly over each side of the fish. Shake off any excess cornflour.

2 Heat a wok over a high heat until it is hot, then add the 3 tablespoons groundnut or vegetable oil. When the oil is slightly smoking, slide the fish into the oil and pan-fry for 2 minutes or until the fillets are golden brown. Carefully turn the fish over and fry the other side. Remove the fish and drain on kitchen paper.

3 Reheat the wok over a high heat until it is hot, then add the 1½ tablespoons groundnut or vegetable oil. When the oil is hot and slightly smoking, add the garlic and ginger and stir-fry for 20 seconds. Then add the rest of the sauce ingredients except the cornflour paste and sesame oil. Stir-fry the sauce for 1 minute, then add the cornflour paste, and when the sauce boils, reduce the heat to low. Carefully slide the fillets into the sauce and cook for 3–5 minutes, basting constantly while cooking.

4 Carefully remove the fish and arrange on a platter. Add the sesame oil to the sauce, then pour over the fish and garnish with chopped spring onions. Serve at once, with fried rice and a vegetable dish.

Sichuan Scallops with Whole Garlic

Da Suan Gan Bei

SERVES: 4

- 1½ tablespoons groundnut or vegetable oil
- ½ teaspoon salt
- ¼ teaspoon freshly ground white pepper
- 8 garlic cloves, peeled but left whole and blanched
- 1 tablespoon peeled and finely chopped fresh root ginger
- 3 shallots or 1 small onion, sliced
- 2 tablespoons Shaoxing rice wine or dry sherry
- 2 tablespoons chicken stock
- 500 g (1 lb) raw shelled scallops, including the corals
- 1 teaspoon chilli bean sauce
- 2 teaspoons dark soy sauce
- 2 teaspoons sugar
- ½ teaspoon chilli oil
- 1 teaspoon sesame oil
- 3 tablespoons finely chopped spring onions, white part only
- ½ teaspoon roasted ground Sichuan peppercorns

Chinese love scallops, and stir-frying prevents them from overcooking while highlighting their distinctive flavour. Here, whole garlic is treated as a vegetable, which makes it wonderfully sweet.

1 Heat a wok over a high heat until it is hot, then add the groundnut or vegetable oil. When the oil is hot and slightly smoking, add the salt, pepper, garlic, ginger and shallots or onion. Stir-fry for 30 seconds, then add the rice wine or sherry and stock. Cook the mixture for 1 minute.

2 Add the scallops and stir-fry for 1 minute. Then add the rest of the ingredients except the spring onions and ground Sichuan peppercorns. Continue to stir-fry for 4 minutes or until the scallops are firm and thoroughly coated with the sauce. Add the spring onions and ground peppercorns and stir-fry for another minute. Serve at once, with rice and a soup for a light meal.

Steamed Salmon
Jeng Sa Men Yu

SERVES: 2–4

625 g (1¼ lb) salmon fillets

1 teaspoon salt

¼ teaspoon freshly ground white pepper

1 tablespoon Shaoxing rice wine or dry sherry

1 tablespoon peeled and finely chopped fresh root ginger

2 teaspoons light soy sauce

2 teaspoons dark soy sauce

3 tablespoons finely chopped spring onions

1 tablespoon groundnut or vegetable oil

2 teaspoons sesame oil

Steaming, a classic Chinese method of cooking fresh fish, preserves the delicate flavours and keeps the flesh moist. The other ingredients here further enhance the noble taste of the salmon.

1 Rub the salmon fillets evenly with the salt and pepper. Place them on a heatproof plate, pour the rice wine or sherry over the fillets and evenly scatter the ginger over the top.

2 Set up a steamer or put a rack into a wok or deep saucepan. Fill the steamer with about 5 cm (2 inches) of hot water. Bring the water to a simmer. Put the plate with the fish into the steamer or onto the rack. Cover the steamer, wok or pan tightly and gently steam over a medium heat for 8–10 minutes, depending on the thickness of the fillets. Replenish the water from time to time.

3 When the fish is cooked, remove the plate from the steamer, wok or pan. Pour the soy sauces evenly over the fish and evenly distribute the spring onions.

4 Heat a wok until it is hot, then add the oils. When the oils are very hot and start to smoke, pour over the fillets. Serve at once, with a stir-fried meat dish, rice and vegetables for an elegant meal.

Vegetables

Four Vegetables in Portuguese Sauce
Pu Zhi Ju Si Shu

SERVES: 4

1½ tablespoons groundnut or vegetable oil

1½ tablespoons peeled and finely chopped fresh root ginger

1 tablespoon finely chopped garlic

1 tablespoon finely chopped spring onions

1 large onion, thinly sliced

500 g (1 lb) Chinese leaves, cut into 5 cm (2 inch) pieces

250 g (8 oz) carrots, peeled and cut into 5 cm (2 inch) pieces

250 g (8 oz) potatoes, peeled and cut into 5 cm (2 inch) pieces

400 ml (14 fl oz) canned coconut milk

1 tablespoon light soy sauce

1 tablespoon dark soy sauce

1 tablespoon Shaoxing rice wine or dry sherry

3 tablespoons Madras curry paste

1 tablespoon sugar

1 teaspoon salt

freshly ground black pepper

chopped spring onions, to garnish

Originating in Portuguese Macao, this vegetable dish is accented with the touch of curry. This recipe makes an excellent vegetarian dish that goes very well with rice.

1 Heat a wok over a high heat until it is hot, then add the oil. When the oil is hot and slightly smoking, add the ginger, garlic and spring onions and stir-fry for 20 seconds. Then add the onion and stir-fry for 2 minutes or until lightly browned and soft. Add the Chinese leaves and stir-fry the mixture for 1 minute, then add the carrots and potatoes. Add the coconut milk and the rest of the ingredients to the wok and bring the mixture to the boil.

2 Transfer the contents of the wok to a saucepan. Cover, reduce the heat and simmer for 30 minutes. Garnish with chopped spring onions and serve at once.

Stir-fried Spinach with Garlic
Chao Weng Cai

SERVES: 2–4

500 g (1 lb) fresh spinach

1½ tablespoons groundnut or vegetable oil

3 garlic cloves, thinly sliced

½ teaspoon salt

1 teaspoon sugar

A favourite green of mine, spinach has sufficient character to marry well with the 'stinking rose' (garlic), and the stir-frying technique retains the taste and freshness of both.

1 Remove and discard the stems from the spinach, then pick over the leaves and wash them well. Leave to drain in a colander.

2 Heat a wok until it is hot, then add the oil. When the oil is hot and slightly smoking, add the garlic and salt and stir-fry for 10 seconds. Immediately add the spinach and continue to stir-fry for 3 minutes over a high heat. Add the sugar and cook for another minute.

3 Remove the spinach to a platter with a slotted spoon. Discard the liquid and serve at once with any fish or meat dish.

Beijing Pan-fried Beancurd

Guo Ta Dou Fu

SERVES: 4

2 x 285 g (9½ oz) packets
  fresh firm tofu
  (beancurd)

cornflour, for dusting

1 egg, beaten

300 ml (½ pint)
  groundnut or
  vegetable oil

2 tablespoons coarsely
  chopped garlic

2 tablespoons peeled
  and finely chopped
  fresh root ginger

3 tablespoons finely
  chopped spring
  onions, white part
  only

3 tablespoons Shaoxing
  rice wine or dry
  sherry

2 tablespoons whole
  bean sauce

1 tablespoon chilli bean
  sauce

2 teaspoons sugar

1 teaspoon salt

150 ml (¼ pint) chicken
  stock, or use wine or
  water for a vegetarian
  version

2 teaspoons sesame oil

Here, tofu is coated with a batter, slowly pan-fried and then braised over a low heat until all the savoury liquid is absorbed as into a sponge.

1 Gently cut the tofu into 5 cm (2 inch) x 2.5 cm (1 inch) x 1 cm (½ inch) pieces and drain on kitchen paper for 10 minutes.

2 Dust the tofu pieces with cornflour, then dip into the beaten egg to coat well. Heat a wok until it is hot, then add the groundnut or vegetable oil. When the oil is hot and slightly smoking, add the tofu pieces and pan-fry for 4–5 minutes until they are golden, then turn over and pan-fry the other side. Drain them well on kitchen paper. Discard all the oil except for 1½ tablespoons.

3 Reheat the wok and oil over a high heat until it is hot. When the oil is hot and slightly smoking, add the garlic and ginger and stir-fry for 1 minute, then add the spring onions and stir-fry for 30 seconds. Return the tofu to the wok, then add the rest of the ingredients and cook for 5 minutes over a low heat until the tofu has absorbed all the liquid.

4 Transfer to a serving platter and serve at once. This dish goes well with noodles or rice, or can be served as a vegetable accompaniment to any meat or fish dishes.

Stir-fried Pak Choi
Chao Bai Cai

SERVES: 4

750 g (1½ lb) pak choi

1 tablespoon groundnut or vegetable oil

1 teaspoon salt

4 garlic cloves, coarsely chopped

In my experience, this is the most delectable way to enjoy pak choi, one of Chinese cuisine's most venerable vegetables, a tasty green that resembles Swiss chard.

1 Separate the individual leaves with stems from the main stem of the pak choi. Cut them into 8 cm (3¼ inch) pieces. Peel the main stems and cut them into the same-sized pieces. Wash the pak choi in several changes of cold water. Drain thoroughly in a colander.

2 Heat a wok over a high heat until it is hot, then add the oil. When the oil is hot and slightly smoking, add the salt and garlic. Stir-fry for 20 seconds or until the garlic begins to brown. Then add the pak choi and continue to stir-fry for 5 minutes over a high heat. Serve at once as a vegetable side dish.

Mixed Green Vegetables
Jiao Wai Cai Yuan

SERVES: 4

1½ tablespoons
  groundnut or
  vegetable oil

6 garlic cloves, crushed

1½ teaspoons salt

½ teaspoon freshly
  ground white pepper

500 g (1 lb) Chinese
  leaves, cut into 5 cm
  (2 inch) pieces
  widthways

200 ml (7 fl oz) chicken
  stock or water

325 g (11 oz) pak choi,
  cut into 5 cm (2 inch)
  pieces widthways

300 g (10 oz) Shanghai
  pak choi (Shanghai
  cabbage), split in half

1 teaspoon cornflour,
  blended with
  2 teaspoons water to
  a smooth paste

This simple recipe is a delicious way to experience Chinese vegetables, first stir-fried, then slowly braised in chicken stock. Shanghai pak choi is sometimes called 'baby pak choi'.

1 Heat a wok over a high heat until it is hot, then add the oil. When the oil is hot and slightly smoking, add the garlic, salt and pepper. Stir-fry for 20 seconds. Then add the Chinese leaves and stock or water and continue to stir-fry for 2 minutes. Add the pak choi and Shanghai pak choi and continue to stir-fry for 2 minutes.

2 Reduce the heat, cover and simmer for 8 minutes. When the vegetables are cooked, remove them to a platter. Increase the heat to high and add the cornflour paste to thicken the stock. Cook for 30 seconds and then pour over the vegetables. Serve at once.

Lettuce with Oyster Sauce
Wo Sun Hao You

SERVES: 4

750 g (1½ lb) iceberg
lettuce (about 1 head)

1 tablespoon groundnut
or vegetable oil

1 teaspoon sesame oil

3 tablespoons oyster
sauce

salt

Oyster sauce, a popular southern Chinese savoury rather than 'fishy' seasoning, melds with hot oils to turn common iceberg lettuce into a delicious vegetable main or side dish.

1 Break the head of lettuce in half with your hands, then separate the lettuce leaves and blanch them in a saucepan of salted boiling water for about 30 seconds. Drain them well in a colander.

2 Heat a wok until it is hot, then add the oils. When the oils are hot and slightly smoking, remove the wok from the heat. Arrange the lettuce leaves on a serving platter, drizzle the oyster sauce evenly over the leaves, then add the hot oils over the top – they will sizzle. Mix well and serve immediately.

Vegetarian Dumplings

Hua Su Jiao

SERVES: 4-6
(MAKES 35-40
DUMPLINGS)

250 g (8 oz) wonton
skins

plain flour, for dusting

1.2 litres (2 pints)
chicken stock or water

chopped spring onions,
to garnish

FILLING

1 tablespoon groundnut
or vegetable oil

2 tablespoons finely
chopped garlic

250 g (8 oz) pak choi,
finely chopped

250 g (8 oz) Chinese
leaves, finely chopped

125 g (4 oz) fresh or
frozen peas

25 g (1 oz) Sichuan
preserved vegetables,
thoroughly rinsed and
finely chopped

2 tablespoons Shaoxing
rice wine or dry
sherry

1 tablespoon dark soy
sauce

2 teaspoons sugar

1 teaspoon sesame oil

1 teaspoon salt

½ teaspoon freshly
ground black pepper

2 tablespoons finely
chopped spring
onions

Dumplings in any form are universally popular in China. In this version, I have used wonton skins, which are simple to use, light and easily available.

1 Heat a wok over a high heat until it is hot, then add the groundnut or vegetable oil. When the oil is hot and slightly smoking, add the garlic and stir-fry for 20 seconds. Then add the pak choi, Chinese leaves, peas and preserved vegetables and continue to stir-fry for 1 minute. Add the rice wine or sherry, soy sauce, sugar, sesame oil, salt and pepper. Continue to cook for 3 minutes, then add the spring onions. Cook for 3 minutes until most of the liquid has evaporated. Put the mixture in a bowl and leave it to cool thoroughly.

2 Put about 1 tablespoon of the filling in the centre of each wonton skin and then fold in half. Moisten the edges with water and pinch together with your fingers. Pleat around the edge, pinching to seal well. Transfer the finished dumplings to a floured tray and keep it covered with a damp cloth until you have filled all the dumplings in this way.

3 When the dumplings are ready, bring the stock or water to a simmer in a large saucepan, add the dumplings and poach for 1 minute or until they float to the surface. Continue to simmer them in the stock for 2 minutes.

TO SERVE

small bowl of white rice vinegar

small bowl of chilli oil

small bowl of dark soy sauce

4 Transfer to a platter. Arrange 3 small bowls, each containing white rice vinegar, chilli oil and dark soy sauce. The idea is to let each person concoct their own dipping sauce by mixing these 3 condiments exactly to their taste. Garnish the dumplings with chopped spring onions and serve at once.

Green Beans with Garlic and Ginger
Chao Yun Dao

SERVES: 4

500 g (1 lb) green beans
or Chinese long beans,
trimmed

1½ tablespoons
groundnut or
vegetable oil

½ teaspoon salt

2 tablespoons finely
chopped garlic

1 teaspoon peeled and
finely chopped fresh
root ginger

100 ml (3½ fl oz) chicken
stock

1 teaspoon sugar

2 teaspoons sesame oil

This is a superb, quick way to cook green beans. The distinctive zest of garlic and ginger goes well with the fresh taste and texture of the beans.

1 If you are using Chinese long beans, cut them into 8 cm (3¼ inch) pieces.

2 Heat a wok until it is hot, then add the groundnut or vegetable oil. When the oil is hot and slightly smoking, add the salt. Then add the garlic and ginger and stir-fry for 10 seconds. Quickly add the beans, stock and sugar and continue to cook for 4 minutes or until the beans are just tender and most of the liquid has evaporated.

3 Stir the sesame oil into the wok and serve the beans at once.

Peanuts with Five-Spice
Wu Xiang Hua Sheng

250 g (8 oz) shelled raw
   peanuts

300 ml (½ pint)
   groundnut or
   vegetable oil

2 tablespoons finely
   chopped garlic

1 tablespoon peeled and
   finely chopped fresh
   root ginger

1 tablespoon sugar

2 teaspoons five-spice
   powder

2 teaspoons salt

1 teaspoon roasted
   ground Sichuan
   peppercorns

1 teaspoon chilli
   powder

This is a way to raise nuts to new, fragrant heights. Serve as a snack with drinks or as an easy addition to any meal. They are best eaten within a day or two of preparation.

1 If the peanuts have their red skins on, immerse in a saucepan of boiling water for about 2 minutes, then drain and leave them to cool, after which the skins will come off easily.

2 Heat a wok over a high heat until it is hot, then add the oil. When the oil is hot and slightly smoking, fry the peanuts for 2 minutes until they are lightly brown. Remove and drain well. Lay the peanuts on a baking sheet lined with kitchen paper.

3 Drain most of the oil from the wok, leaving just 1½ tablespoons (the remaining oil can be saved for future use). Reheat the wok and the oil, and when it is hot and smoking slightly, add the garlic and ginger and stir-fry for 1 minute. Then add the rest of the ingredients and return the peanuts to the wok. Continue to stir-fry for 2 minutes, stirring to mix well. Turn onto a baking sheet, leave to cool and then serve.

Fish-flavoured Aubergine
Yu Xiang Qie Zi

750 g (1½ lb) medium
aubergines

400 ml (14 fl oz)
groundnut or
vegetable oil

2 tablespoons finely
chopped garlic

2 tablespoons peeled
and finely chopped
fresh root ginger

3 tablespoons finely
chopped spring
onions

chopped spring onions,
to garnish

SAUCE

1½ tablespoons dark
soy sauce

2 tablespoons Shaoxing
rice wine or dry
sherry

2 tablespoons black rice
vinegar

1½ tablespoons sugar

1 tablespoon roasted
Sichuan peppercorns,
crushed

2 teaspoons chilli bean
sauce

125 ml (4 fl oz) chicken
stock

*This dish doesn't taste 'fishy'; rather, the spices and seasonings create
the flavours usually employed when preparing fish: hot, sour, salty
and sweet at the same time.*

1 Cut the aubergines into 8 cm x 5 mm (3¼ x ¼ inch) pieces.

2 Heat a wok until it is hot, then add the oil. When the
oil is hot and slightly smoking, deep-fry the aubergines in
several batches. Remove them with a slotted spoon and
drain them well on kitchen paper.

3 Pour off most of the oil, leaving 2 tablespoons, and
reheat the wok. When it is hot, add the garlic, ginger
and spring onions and stir-fry for 30 seconds. Add all the
sauce ingredients except the stock. Continue to cook for
2 minutes over a high heat, then add the stock and simmer
for another 3 minutes. Return the aubergine to the wok
and simmer in the sauce for 3 minutes.

4 Turn onto a platter, garnish with chopped spring onions
and serve at once.

Spicy Sichuan Beancurd
Ma Po Dou Fu

SERVES: 2 – 4

2 x 285 g (9½ oz) packets silken (soft) tofu (beancurd)

2 tablespoons groundnut or vegetable oil

250 g (8 oz) minced beef

2 tablespoons coarsely chopped garlic

2 tablespoons chilli bean sauce

1 tablespoon dark soy sauce

1 tablespoon Shaoxing rice wine or dry sherry

2 teaspoons sugar

½ teaspoon salt

150 ml (¼ pint) chicken stock or water

2 teaspoons roasted ground Sichuan peppercorns

2 teaspoons sesame oil

The essence of this recipe lies in the seasonings and condiments; their quality and the care taken in cooking them just right – one of the most delicious ways to enjoy tofu.

1 Gently cut the tofu into 1 cm (½ inch) cubes and drain on kitchen paper for 10 minutes.

2 Heat a wok until it is hot, then add the groundnut or vegetable oil. When the oil is hot and slightly smoking, add the beef and stir-fry for 2 minutes to partially cook. Add the garlic and stir-fry for 1 minute. Then add the chilli bean sauce and soy sauce and continue to stir-fry for another minute. Add the rice wine or sherry, sugar and salt and continue to stir-fry for 30 seconds.

3 Add the stock or water and the tofu to the wok and cook for 3 minutes over a high heat. Then stir in the ground Sichuan peppercorns and sesame oil. Ladle the mixture into a serving bowl and serve with rice.

Beancurd with Minced Pork
Dou Fu Rou Song

2 x 285 g (9½ oz) packets
firm tofu (beancurd)

1½ tablespoons
groundnut or
vegetable oil

2 tablespoons finely
chopped garlic

2 tablespoons finely
chopped shallots

2 tablespoons finely
chopped spring
onions, white
part only

2 teaspoons peeled and
finely chopped fresh
root ginger

375 g (12 oz) minced
pork

2 teaspoons whole
yellow bean sauce

1 tablespoon chilli bean
sauce

1 tablespoon dark soy
sauce

1 tablespoon light soy
sauce

1 tablespoon Shaoxing
rice wine or dry
sherry

150 ml (¼ pint) chicken
stock or water

2 teaspoons sugar

freshly ground black
pepper

chopped spring onions,
to garnish

*This home-cooked dish is easy and tasty, using a small amount of
meat to flavour versatile tofu, along with a variety of spices and
flavours that it also absorbs.*

1 Gently cut the tofu into 2.5 cm (1 inch) cubes and drain
on kitchen paper for 10 minutes.

2 Heat a wok until it is hot, then add the oil. When the
oil is hot and slightly smoking, add the garlic, shallots,
spring onion and ginger and stir-fry for 30 seconds. Then
add the pork, stir well to break up all the pieces and
continue to stir-fry for 2 minutes or until it loses its pink
colour. Remove any excess fat. Add the bean sauces, soy
sauces, rice wine or sherry, stock or water, sugar and
pepper to taste and continue to cook for 30 seconds.

3 Add the tofu to the wok and cook over a high heat
for 2 minutes, gently mixing well. Continue to cook for
4 minutes or until most of the liquid has evaporated. Turn
onto a platter, garnish with chopped spring onions and
serve at once. This dish goes well with rice.

Twice-fried Green Beans
Gan Bian Si Ji Dou

SERVES: 4

**600 ml (1 pint)
groundnut or
vegetable oil**

**500 g (1 lb) Chinese long
beans or runner
beans, trimmed**

**3 tablespoons finely
chopped spring
onions**

**2 tablespoons finely
chopped garlic**

**1 tablespoon peeled and
finely chopped fresh
root ginger**

**2 tablespoons chilli
bean sauce**

**1 tablespoon whole
yellow bean sauce**

**2 tablespoons Shaoxing
rice wine or dry
sherry**

**1 tablespoon dark soy
sauce**

2 teaspoons sugar

**2 teaspoons roasted
ground Sichuan
peppercorns**

**2 tablespoons water or
chicken stock**

This involves two procedures: deep-frying, which accentuates textures, and stir-frying in spicy aromatic seasonings, which transforms the dish into a tempting one even for non-vegetarians.

1 Heat a wok over a high heat until it is hot, then add the oil. When the oil is hot and slightly smoking, add the beans, in 2 or 3 batches at a time, and deep-fry for 3 minutes or until deep green and slightly wrinkled. Remove the beans and drain them well in a colander. Lay them on a baking sheet lined with kitchen paper.

2 Drain off and discard all but 1½ tablespoons of the oil (or save the oil for future stir-frying of vegetables). Reheat the wok and oil over a high heat, and when it is hot, add the spring onions, garlic and ginger and stir-fry for 30 seconds. Add the bean sauces, rice wine or sherry, soy sauce, sugar and ground Sichuan peppercorns and stir-fry for 1 minute. Return the beans to the wok, add the water or stock and continue to stir-fry for another 2 minutes or until the beans are thoroughly coated with the sauce and are heated through. Serve at once, with meat or fish dishes.

Cold Pepper with Black Beans
Jiao Ban Xing Jiao

SERVES: 4

1½ tablespoons groundnut or vegetable oil

3 tablespoons finely chopped shallots

2 tablespoons coarsely chopped black beans

1½ tablespoons finely chopped garlic

1 tablespoon peeled and finely chopped fresh root ginger

175 g (6 oz) red peppers, cored, deseeded and cut into 2.5 x 2.5 cm (1 x 1 inch) pieces

175 g (6 oz) yellow peppers, cored, deseeded and cut into 2.5 x 2.5 cm (1 x 1 inch) pieces

175 g (6 oz) green peppers, cored, deseeded and cut into 2.5 x 2.5 cm (1 x 1 inch) pieces

2 tablespoons Shaoxing rice wine or dry sherry

1 tablespoon chilli bean sauce

2 tablespoons dark soy sauce

1 tablespoon light soy sauce

2 teaspoons sugar

150 ml (¼ pint) chicken stock or water

2 teaspoons sesame oil

The black beans add a pungent aroma and delectable flavour to this vegetarian dish. The peppers taste even better if you let them stand for 2 hours before serving.

1 Heat a wok over a high heat until it is hot, then add the groundnut or vegetable oil. When the oil is hot and slightly smoking, add the shallots, black beans, garlic and ginger and stir-fry for 1 minute. Then add the peppers and stir-fry for 1 minute. Finally, add the rice wine or sherry, chilli bean sauce, soy sauces, sugar and stock or water.

2 Continue to cook over a high heat for 5 minutes or until the peppers are soft and most of the liquid has evaporated. Stir in the sesame oil and give the mixture several stirs to mix well. Turn onto a platter and leave to cool. Serve at room temperature.

Crispy 'Seaweed'
Zha Cai

SERVES: 4

1.1 kg (2¼ lb) pak choi

900 ml (1½ pints) groundnut or vegetable oil

1 teaspoon salt

2 teaspoons sugar

50 g (2 oz) pine kernels, lightly roasted, to garnish

Pak choi substitutes well for the special type of seaweed used in this eastern-northern dish in China, now so popular in the West, or try the recipe with spinach leaves.

1 Separate the individual leaves with stems from the main stem of the pak choi and cut the green leaves from the white stems (save the stems and stir-fry them with garlic or use them for soup). Wash the green leaves in several changes of cold water. Drain them thoroughly in a colander and spin them dry in a salad spinner.

2 Take the leaves, roll them up tightly and finely shred them. Lay them out to dry on a baking sheet and then put them in a preheated oven, 120°C (250°F), Gas Mark ½, for 15 minutes to dry. Remove from the oven and leave to cool. This can be done the day before.

3 Heat a wok over a high heat until it is hot, then add the oil. When the oil is hot and slightly smoking, deep-fry the greens, in 2 or 3 batches, for about 30 seconds until they turn deep green, then remove them immediately and drain well on kitchen paper. Leave to cool.

4 Toss the crispy greens in the salt and sugar. Garnish with the pine kernels and serve.

Rice & Noodles

Stir-fried Egg Noodles

Chao Lao Mian

SERVES: 4

2.25 litres (4 pints)
  water

2 teaspoons salt

250 g (8 oz) fresh or
  dried egg noodles

1½ tablespoons
  groundnut or
  vegetable oil

2 tablespoons finely
  chopped garlic

6 whole spring onions,
  finely shredded

4 slices of fresh root
  ginger, peeled and
  finely shredded

175 g (6 oz) cooked ham,
  shredded

175 g (6 oz) fresh bean
  sprouts

1 tablespoon light soy
  sauce

1 tablespoon Shaoxing
  rice wine or dry
  sherry

2 teaspoons sugar

3½ tablespoons oyster
  sauce

2 teaspoons sesame oil,
  plus extra for tossing
  with the noodles
  (optional)

freshly ground black
  pepper

Perhaps the most popular Chinese dish in the world, this 'chow mein' can be made vegetarian by eliminating the ham, or substitute fish, prawns or other meat.

1 Put the water and salt into a large saucepan and bring to the boil. Add the noodles. If you are using fresh noodles, boil them for 1½ minutes; if using dried noodles, boil them for 3 minutes. Separate the noodles, using chopsticks, while they are boiling. Put them in a colander under cold running water and leave until they are cold, to stop them from overcooking. Leave the noodles to drain in the colander, turning them several times so that all the water can drain off them. If you are not using them immediately, toss them with sesame oil before setting aside.

2 Heat a wok until it is hot, then add the groundnut or vegetable oil. When the oil is hot and slightly smoking, add the garlic, spring onions and ginger and stir-fry for 30 seconds. Then add the ham, bean sprouts, soy sauce, rice wine or sherry, sugar and pepper to taste and continue to cook for 30 seconds, mixing well.

3 Return the noodles to the wok and cook over a high heat for 2 minutes, mixing well. Stir in oyster sauce and sesame oil and continue to stir-fry for 2 minutes. Turn onto a platter and serve at once.

Plain Boiled Rice
Si Miao Bai Fun

SERVES: 4-6

enough long-grain rice to fill a glass measuring jug to 400 ml (14 fl oz)

600 ml (1 pint) water

This is an easy and foolproof basic rice recipe that always produces excellent results. The required rice is simple long-grain rice, of which there are many varieties.

1 Put the rice into a large bowl and wash it in several changes of water until the water becomes clear (this step may be omitted if you are in a hurry, with no significant adverse consequences). Drain the rice and put it into a heavy saucepan with the water – the water should be 2.5 cm (1 inch) above the surface of the rice; too much water means gummy rice. Bring it to the boil over a high heat and continue boiling until all the surface liquid has evaporated. This should take about 15 minutes. The surface of the rice should have small indentations like pitted craters.

2 At this point, cover the pan with a very tight-fitting lid, reduce the heat as low as possible and let the rice cook undisturbed for 15 minutes – never uncover the pan once the simmering process has begun. Remove from the heat and leave the rice to rest for 5 minutes before serving.

Sichuan Spicy Noodles
Dan Dan Mian

SERVES: 4

2.25 litres (4 pints) water

2 teaspoons salt

250 g (8 oz) fresh or dried egg noodles

1½ tablespoons groundnut oil

3 tablespoons finely chopped garlic

2 tablespoons peeled and finely chopped fresh root ginger

4 tablespoons finely chopped spring onions (white part)

375 g (12 oz) minced pork

2 tablespoons sesame paste or peanut butter

2 tablespoons dark soy sauce

2 tablespoons chilli oil

1 tablespoon chilli bean sauce

1 tablespoon sugar

2 teaspoons salt

175 ml (6 fl oz) chicken stock

1 tablespoon Sichuan peppercorns, roasted and ground

2 teaspoons sesame oil, plus extra for tossing with the noodles (optional)

freshly ground black pepper

chopped spring onions, to garnish

This typical Sichuan dish is now popular throughout China, especially in the north. If you prefer it less oily, halve the chilli oil and exclude the sesame oil.

1 Put the water and salt into a large saucepan and bring to the boil. Add the noodles. If you are using fresh noodles, boil them for 1½ minutes; if using dried noodles, boil them for 3 minutes. Separate the noodles, using chopsticks, while they are boiling. Put them in a colander under cold running water and leave until they are cold, to stop them overcooking. Let the noodles drain in the colander, turning them several times so that all the water can drain off them. If you are not using them immediately, toss them with sesame oil before setting aside.

2 Heat a wok until it is hot, then add the groundnut or vegetable oil. When the oil is hot and slightly smoking, add the garlic, ginger and spring onions and stir-fry for 30 seconds. Then add the pork, stir well to break up all the pieces and continue to stir-fry for 2 minutes or until it loses its pink colour. Add the rest of the ingredients, except the sesame oil, with black pepper to taste and continue to cook for 5 minutes.

3 Return the noodles to the wok and heat for 2 minutes, mixing well. Stir in the sesame oil and mix. Turn onto a platter, garnish with chopped spring onions and serve at once.

Fried Rice

Chao Fan

SERVES: 4 – 6

2 eggs, beaten

2 teaspoons sesame oil

1½ teaspoons salt

1½ tablespoons
groundnut or
vegetable oil

Plain Boiled Rice, cold
(see page 144)

175 g (6 oz) cooked ham
or lean smoked bacon,
diced

6 tablespoons finely
chopped spring
onions

175 g (6 oz) fresh bean
sprouts

For perfect fried rice, use cold cooked rice, and make sure that the wok is very hot before adding the oil. Add your favourite ingredients or any leftovers.

1 Combine the beaten eggs, sesame oil and 1 teaspoon of the salt and set aside.

2 Heat a wok until it is hot, then add the groundnut or vegetable oil. When the oil is hot and slightly smoking, add the rice and stir-fry for 1 minute. Then add the ham or bacon, spring onions and the remaining salt. Continue to stir-fry for 3 minutes and then add the egg mixture. Stir-fry for 2 minutes and then add the bean sprouts. Mix well and stir-fry for another 2 minutes or until the bean sprouts are heated through.

3 Turn onto a platter and serve at once.

Bean Sauce Noodles
Zha Jiang Mian

SERVES: 4

2.25 litres (4 pints) water

2 teaspoons salt

250 g (8 oz) fresh or dried egg noodles

1½ tablespoons groundnut or vegetable oil

2 tablespoons finely chopped garlic

2 tablespoons finely chopped spring onions, white part only

2 teaspoons peeled and finely chopped fresh root ginger

375 g (12 oz) minced pork

2 teaspoons ground yellow bean sauce

1 tablespoon chilli bean sauce

1 tablespoon dark soy sauce

1 tablespoon light soy sauce

1 tablespoon Shaoxing rice wine or dry sherry

150 ml (¼ pint) chicken stock

2 teaspoons sugar

2 teaspoons sesame oil, plus extra for tossing with the noodles (optional)

freshly ground black pepper

chopped spring onions, to garnish

This northern Chinese dish is perhaps best described as the equivalent of Western pasta with meat sauce. With added vegetables, it makes a very satisfying light meal or snack.

1 Put the water and salt into a large saucepan and bring to the boil. Add the noodles. If you are using fresh noodles, boil them for 1½ minutes; if using dried noodles, boil them for 3 minutes. Separate the noodles, using chopsticks, while they are boiling. Put them in a colander under cold running water and leave until they are cold, to stop them from overcooking. Leave the noodles to drain in the colander, turning them several times so that all the water can drain off them. If you are not using them immediately, toss them with sesame oil before setting aside.

2 Heat a wok until it is hot, then add the groundnut or vegetable oil. When the oil is hot and slightly smoking, add the garlic, spring onions and ginger and stir-fry for 30 seconds. Then add the pork, stir well to break up all the pieces and continue to stir-fry for 2 minutes or until it loses its pink colour. Add the bean sauces, soy sauces, rice wine or sherry, stock, sugar and pepper to taste and continue to cook for 30 seconds, mixing well.

3 Return the noodles to the wok and cook over a high heat for 2 minutes, mixing well. Stir in the sesame oil and mix again. Turn onto a platter, garnish with chopped spring onions and serve at once.

Noodles in Curry Sauce
San Zhi Mian

SERVES: 4

2.25 litres (4 pints) water

2 teaspoons salt

250 g (8 oz) fresh or dried egg noodles

sesame oil, for tossing with the noodles (optional)

1½ tablespoons groundnut or vegetable oil

2 tablespoons finely chopped garlic

2 tablespoons finely chopped spring onions, white part only

2 teaspoons peeled and finely chopped fresh root ginger

375 g (12 oz) minced pork

2 tablespoons Madras curry paste

1 tablespoon chilli bean sauce

1 tablespoon dark soy sauce

1 tablespoon light soy sauce

1 tablespoon Shaoxing rice wine

150 ml (¼ pint) chicken stock

150 ml (¼ pint) coconut milk

2 teaspoons sugar

freshly ground black pepper

chopped spring onions, to garnish

Chinese cuisine readily adopts new foods and ingredients when their virtues are recognized, as in the case of curry. These noodles are tasty enough to eat on their own.

1 Put the water and salt into a large saucepan and bring to the boil. Add the noodles. If you are using fresh noodles, boil them for 1½ minutes; if using dried noodles, boil them for 3 minutes. Separate the noodles, using chopsticks, while they are boiling. Put them in a colander under cold running water and leave until they are cold, to stop them from overcooking. Leave the noodles to drain in the colander, turning them several times so that all the water can drain off them. If you are not using them immediately, toss them with sesame oil before setting aside.

2 Heat a wok until it is hot, then add the groundnut or vegetable oil. When the oil is hot and slightly smoking, add the garlic, spring onions and ginger and stir-fry for 30 seconds. Then add the pork, stir well to break up all the pieces and continue to stir-fry for 2 minutes or until it loses its pink colour. Add the rest of the ingredients with pepper to taste and continue to cook over a high heat for 2 minutes.

3 Return the noodles to the wok and cook over a high heat for 2 minutes, mixing well. Turn onto a platter, garnish with chopped spring onions and serve at once.

Stir-fried Rice Noodles
Chao Fen

SERVES: 4

250 g (8 oz) dried rice
noodles, round or flat

1½ tablespoons
groundnut or
vegetable oil

1 small onion, thinly
sliced

1 large red chilli,
deseeded and thinly
sliced

2 tablespoons finely
chopped garlic

1 green pepper, cored,
deseeded and thinly
shredded

2 tablespoons light soy
sauce

1 tablespoon Shaoxing
rice wine or dry
sherry

2 tablespoons Madras
curry paste

2 teaspoons sugar

1 teaspoon salt

125 ml (4 fl oz) chicken
stock

1 egg, beaten

125 g (4 oz) cooked
peeled prawns,
deveined and coarsely
chopped

3 tablespoons finely
chopped spring
onions

*Rice noodles are very popular in eastern and southern China.
This favourite recipe, flavoured with curry, was brought to
China by returning immigrants from Singapore.*

1 Soak the noodles in warm water for 15 minutes or until
they are soft. Drain the noodles thoroughly in a colander
and set aside.

2 Heat a wok over a high heat until it is hot, then add
the oil. When the oil is hot and slightly smoking, add
the onion, chilli and garlic and stir-fry for 1 minute. Then
add the green pepper, noodles, soy sauce, rice wine or
sherry, curry paste, sugar, salt and stock. Cook the mixture
over a high heat for 5 minutes until most of the liquid
has evaporated.

3 Add the beaten egg and prawns to the wok and continue
to stir-fry for another minute, mixing well. Finally, add
the spring onions. Give the mixture several good stirs and
serve at once.

Crispy Noodles with Spicy Pork
Ma Yi Shang Shu

SERVES: 4

125 g (4 oz) dried bean thread noodles

400 ml (14 fl oz) groundnut or vegetable oil, plus 1 tablespoon

250 g (8 oz) minced pork

1 tablespoon dark soy sauce

2 teaspoons Shaoxing rice wine or dry sherry

2 teaspoons sesame oil

1 tablespoon peeled and chopped fresh root ginger

2 tablespoons finely chopped garlic

4 tablespoons finely chopped spring onions

2 teaspoons dark soy sauce

2 teaspoons light soy sauce

1 tablespoon chilli bean sauce

1 teaspoon roasted ground Sichuan peppercorns

chopped spring onions, to garnish

I particularly like this version out of many of this Sichuan dish, where the noodles are fried first, resulting in a crispy texture complemented by the spicy sauce.

1 Separate and break the noodles up in a paper bag, to stop them flying all over the place.

2 Heat a wok until it is hot, then add the 400 ml (14 fl oz) groundnut or vegetable oil. When the oil is hot and slightly smoking, deep-fry the bean thread noodles in several batches. They will immediately puff up and triple their volume. Remove them quickly with a slotted spoon and drain over kitchen paper. Set the noodles aside and wipe the wok clean. Strain the oil through a fine sieve and store for reusing.

3 Combine the pork with the soy sauce, rice wine or sherry and sesame oil in a bowl.

4 Reheat the wok until it is hot, then add the remaining 1 tablespoon groundnut or vegetable oil. When the oil is hot and slightly smoking, add the ginger, garlic and spring onions and stir-fry for 20 seconds. Then add the pork mixture and stir-fry for 2 minutes. Add the rest of the ingredients and bring the mixture to a simmer. Mix well and continue to cook over a high heat for about 5 minutes.

5 Add the fried noodles to the wok and mix quickly. Ladle into a large serving bowl, garnish with chopped spring onions and serve immediately.

Beef Fried Rice

Niu Rou Chao Fan

SERVES: 4−6

250 g (8 oz) minced beef

1 egg, beaten

1 teaspoon sesame oil

3 tablespoons groundnut or vegetable oil

2 tablespoons finely chopped garlic

1 tablespoon peeled and finely chopped fresh root ginger

Plain Boiled Rice, cold (see page 144)

6 tablespoons finely chopped spring onions

salt

MARINADE

1 teaspoon light soy sauce

1 teaspoon dark soy sauce

1 teaspoon Shaoxing rice wine or dry sherry

1 teaspoon sesame oil

½ teaspoon salt

½ teaspoon sugar

¼ teaspoon freshly ground black pepper

An appetizing fried rice variation that draws its flavours from the minced beef. It is easy to make, as well as delicious to eat.

1 Combine the beef with all the marinade ingredients in a bowl.

2 In a small bowl, combine the beaten egg, sesame oil and ¼ teaspoon salt and set aside.

3 Heat a wok until it is hot, then add the groundnut or vegetable oil. When the oil is hot and slightly smoking, add the garlic and ginger and stir-fry for 1 minute. Then add the beef and stir-fry for 2 minutes. Add the rice and continue to stir-fry for another 3 minutes. Add the egg mixture and stir-fry for another minute.

4 Give the mixture several good stirs to mix well, add the spring onions and stir again to mix well. Add salt to taste. Turn onto a platter and serve at once.

Chicken and Rice Casserole
Hua Ji Fan

SERVES: 2–4

enough long-grain rice
to fill a glass
measuring jug to
400 ml (14 fl oz)

600 ml (1 pint) chicken
stock

250 g (8 oz) boneless,
skinless chicken
thighs, cut into 2.5 cm
(1 inch) pieces

1½ tablespoons
groundnut or
vegetable oil

1 tablespoon peeled and
finely chopped fresh
root ginger

2 teaspoons finely
chopped garlic

2 tablespoons oyster
sauce

chopped spring onions,
to garnish

MARINADE

1 tablespoon light soy
sauce

2 teaspoons dark soy
sauce

1 tablespoon rice wine
or dry sherry

1 teaspoon salt

2 teaspoons sesame oil

1 teaspoon cornflour

This quick and easy recipe has been popular for many centuries. The rice is cooked in chicken stock, then permeated with the juices and marinade from stir-fried chicken.

1 Put the rice into a large bowl and wash it in several changes of water until the water becomes clear (this step may be omitted if you are in a hurry, with no significant adverse consequences). Drain the rice and put it into a heavy saucepan with the stock. Bring it to the boil over a high heat and continue boiling until all the surface liquid has evaporated. This should take about 15 minutes. The surface of the rice should have small indentations like pitted craters.

2 At this point, cover the pan with a very tight-fitting lid, reduce the heat as low as possible and let the rice cook undisturbed for 15 minutes.

3 Put the chicken and all the marinade ingredients into a glass bowl and mix well. Cover with clingfilm and leave to marinate for 15 minutes. Drain the chicken well, reserving the marinade liquid.

4 Heat a wok over a high heat until it is hot, then add the oil. When the oil is hot and slightly smoking, add the ginger and garlic and stir-fry for 20 seconds. Then add the chicken and stir-fry for 3 minutes or until lightly browned. Add the oyster sauce and reserved marinade liquid and cook for 1 minute, mixing well.

5 Put the chicken and sauce on top of the cooked rice and continue to cook, covered, for 10 minutes. Turn onto a platter, garnish with chopped spring onions and serve at once, with a vegetable dish.

Index

Acknowledgements

Executive Editor: Eleanor Maxfield
Senior Editor: Charlotte Macey
Creative Director: Tracy Killick
Design concept: Smith & Gilmour
Designer: Grade Design
Photographer: Noel Murphy
Home Economist: Sue Henderson
Home Economist's Assistant: Rachel Wood
Stylist: Wei Tang
Senior Production Controller: Amanda Mackie